BEHIND

WHAT THE BIBLE ASSUMES THAT YOU ALREADY KNOW

(Collected Essays)

Gary G Michuta

Unless otherwise indicated, all Scripture quotations in this book are taken from the *New American Bible with Revised New Testament and Revised Psalms* © 1991, 1986, 1970 Confraternity of Christian Doctrine, Washington, D. C. All Rights Reserved. No part of the *New American Bible* may be reproduced in any form without permission in writing from the copyright owner.

Articles from The Michigan Catholic Newspaper reprinted with permission.

BEHIND THE BIBLE: WHAT THE BIBLE ASSUMES THAT YOU ALREADY KNOW

© 2017 by Gary G. Michuta. All rights reserved.

Published by Nikaria Press

Livonia, Michigan

www.HandsOnApologetics.com

Printed in the United States of America

Library of Congress Cataloguing-in-Publication Data

Michuta, Gary G., 1964 -

ISBN-10: 0998839957

ISBN-13: 9780998839950

Contents

INTRODUCTION 11

OLD TESTAMENT 13

   A Brief Look at Biblical Time (October 27, 2016) 13

   Why Did the Authors of the Bible Cite Non-biblical Sources? (June 10, 2016) 15

   Genesis 1 - 2 (Wisdom 11:18): The "First Creation" and the "Second Creation": An Often Forgotten Distinction (April 25, 2017) 19

   Genesis 3:7 - Adam and the Fig Leaf: An Uncomfortable Wardrobe Choice (June 26, 2015) 21

   Genesis 6:5, 12 - Noah, the Flood, and Creation in Reverse (September 30, 2016) 24

   Genesis 9:3-5 - Why Did the Old Covenant Forbid Blood? (July 25, 2014) 26

   Exodus 3:7-8 - Why the 10 Plagues on Egypt? (August 18, 2016) 29

   Exodus 15:26 - The Healing "Code" of the Earliest Christians (October 20, 2015) 31

   Exodus 34:29-30 - Unveiling Moses (June 30, 2017) 34

Deuteronomy 37

   Deuteronomy 28:66 - The Cross and the Old Testament (February 23, 2017) 37

Esther 41

   Esther's Rocky Journey to the Bible (Feb. 5, 2015) 41

THE PROPHETS 45

    Ezekiel 1:1 - Spinning Ezekiel's wheels (October 14, 2016) 45

    Zechariah 12:10-11 - Losing King Josiah: How the disciples mourned when Christ was pierced (May 29, 2015) 47

    Malachi 1:11 - "From the Rising of the Sun...": Every Mass is a Prophecy Fulfilled (May 12, 2016) 50

Song of Songs 53

    The "Song of Songs" Journey to the Bible (Jan. 25, 2016) 53

THE DEUTEROCANON 57

    Did the Jews Ever Accept the Deuterocanon? (November 10, 2016) 57

    Who Wrote the Books of Solomon? (October 30, 2014) 59

    Wisdom 7:27 - The Wisdom behind "God from God, Light from Light" (June 27, 2014) 62

    Wisdom 8:1 - The Wisdom of Science (December 8, 2016) 64

THE NEW TESTAMENT 67

    The Four Gospels: What Sets Them Apart from the Rest? 67

    Which Old Testament Did Jesus Use, Anyway? (December 12, 2014) 69

The Gospel According to Matthew 73

    Matthew 2:16 - Did Herod Slaughter the Holy Innocents? (December 21, 2016) 73

    Matthew 1:23 - Who was to Conceive: A Virgin or a Simply a 'Young Maiden"? (Dec. 22, 2015) 75

Matthew 1:25 - Small Words Can Cause Big Problems (March 31, 2015) 78

Matthew 4:1-11 - Why Did Jesus Fast for 40 Days in the Desert? (February 18, 2016) 80

Matthew 8:24-28 - Master of the Seas: Who Calms the Waters? (November 13, 2015) 82

Matthew 12:32 - Why is Speaking Against the Holy Spirit an Unforgivable Sin? (Dec. 10, 2015) 85

Matthew 4:15-16 - Finding Peter's House (August 8, 2016) ... 87

Matthew 6:12 (Luke 11:4) - The Economics of Sin (July 14, 2017) 90

Matthew 9:20-21 - The Truth About Tassels: Healing Those On The Fringe (November 23, 2016) 92

Matthew 16:18 - "You are Peter...": The Rocky Background to Jesus' words (October 5, 2015) 95

Matthew 16:19 - The Key to Understanding the Papacy (Sept. 5, 2014) 98

Matthew 16:19 - No Need to Get Tied Up with "Binding and Loosing" (August 20, 2015) 100

Matthew 21:11 - What's So Great About Galilee? (July 28, 2017) 102

Matthew 22:24-29 (also, Mark 12:18-29 and Luke 20:27-40) - An Odd Challenge: Seven Marriages to Seven Brothers (March 6, 2015) 105

Matthew 23:35 - Did John the Baptist's Father Die a Martyr? (September 2, 2016) 108

Matthew 24:30, 32 - The End was Near? Scripture's Take on the Last Day (August 10, 2014) 110

Matthew 26:61, Also Mark 14:58 - Sacred Ground: Is the body Really a Temple? (November 14, 2014) 112

The Gospel According to Mark 117

    The Preaching Gospel: Mark's Off-the-cuff Style (November 26, 2014) 117

    Mark 1:1-4 - The Mysterious John the Baptist (February 5, 2016) 119

    Mark 4:1-11 - Christ's Fast in the Desert is an Answer to Israel's History (March 24, 2017) 122

    Mark 3:14 - The Holy Dozen: Why Twelve Apostles and Not Thirteen? (November 24, 2015) 124

    Mark 14:50-52 - The Naked Truth about the Young Man in Mark (Jan. 9, 2015) 127

    Mark 14:62 - What's Behind the High Priest's "Overreaction?" 129

The Gospel According to Luke 133

    Just What the Doctor Ordered: St. Luke the Physician (Sept. 19, 2014) 133

    Luke 1:28 - Is Mary Full of Grace, or Just Highly Favored? (May 30, 2014) 135

    Luke 1:39-43, 56 - Seeing Mary as the Ark of the Covenant (Dec. 26, 2014) 138

    Luke 1:48 - Mary, Jerusalem, and the Problem of Praise (June 12, 2015) 141

- Luke 1:71-74 - Total Recall: Early Christian Memory Devices in the Benedictus (July 10, 2014) 143
- Luke 11:50 (Matthew 23:35) - Did Jesus Give Us Bible Bookends? 146

The Gospel According to John 151

- John 1:1 - The Genesis of John's Prologue: The Background Behind "the Word" 151
- John 1:45-50 - In Nathaniel's Calling, There's More Than Meets the Eye (January 13, 2017) 153
- John 2:6 - What was so Funny at the Wedding at Cana? (Feb. 20, 2015) 156
- John 4:4-30 - Finding a Bride at a Local Watering Hole (September 4, 2015) 158
- John 4:17-18 - Who were the Samaritan Woman's Five Husbands? (April 28, 2016) 161
- John 7:37 - From Spring to King: How Jesus' "living water" Proclaimed His Identity (March 4, 2016) 163
- John 8:1-11 - Getting Caught in Your Own Trap (June 12, 2014) 166
- John 8:51-58 - Who was the 'Third Man" Who Visited Abraham? (September 18, 2015) 168
- John 10:16 - Who are the 'Other Sheep" Jesus Says Belongs to Him? (Aug. 7, 2015) 171
- John 20:21-23 - Did the Apostles Forgive Sins or Just Proclaim Forgiveness (May 1, 2015) 174
- John 21:15-17 - When a Fisherman Became A Shepherd (June 24, 2016) 176

The Acts of the Apostles 179

    Acts 5:35-39 - Christ was Killed; Why weren't His Followers Dispersed? (April 4, 2016) 179

    Acts 7:59 - When the Cat's Away: The Background to St. Stephen's Martyrdom (Oct. 16, 2014) 182

    Acts 18:3 - No Town Like His Hometown: How St. Paul's Shaped His Life (August 22, 2014) 184

    Acts 19:8-12 - No Luck Evangelizing? Try St. Paul Method (March 21, 2016)..187

The Epistles of St. Paul 191

    Romans 4:1-4 - Was Abraham a Jew or a Gentile? (July 13, 2015)...191

    Galatians 3:26-29 - Who is the Blessed Offspring of Abraham? (October 30, 2015) 193

    Ephesians 2:15 - Getting into Trouble with the Law (September 16, 2016) 196

    Philippians 1:27-30 - Onward Christian Soldiers of Philippi (March 9, 2017) 198

    1 Corinthian 5:21 - "If He Makes Himself An Offering for Sin..." (April 7, 2017) 201

    1 Corinthians 15:3 - Discovering early evidence for the resurrection (May 15, 2014)...204

    1 Timothy 4:14 - The Jewish Roots of the Laying on of Hands (July 22, 2016)..207

    Titus 1:12 - The Truth About Cretans (June 8, 2017) 209

The Epistle To the Hebrews...213

Who Wrote Hebrews? (June 22, 2017) 213

Hebrews 4:12 - Is the Bible a "Two-edged Sword"? (April 17, 2015) 215

James 5:2-3 - Get Rid of Your Rusty Gold and Silver (Jan. 8, 2016) 218

The Book of Revelation 223

A Revealing look at Revelation's Journey to the New Testament (July 8, 2016) 223

Revelation 2:17- Jesus and the Sign of the "Hidden Manna" (April 15, 2016) 225

Revelation 1:17 (also Revelation 21:6-7) - Who is the Alpha and the Omega? (May 27, 2016) 228

Revelation 13:18 - The Number of the Beast: What's Behind "666"? (May 8, 2017) 230

Revelation 13:18 - Does "666" Add Up To Nero? (May 18, 2017) 233

INTRODUCTION

Back in 2014, I was approached to write a column for the *Michigan Catholic Newspaper*, an official publication of the Archdiocese of Detroit. The newspaper had recently decided to change its format so as to encourage and support the "New Evangelization." I just missed the chance to write a column on apologetics (the honor was given to my good friend and apologetics devotee David Armstrong), but they needed someone to write a column tackling the Bible in a new and unique way. The idea was to look at the background behind the books of Scripture (i.e., things like the formation of the canon and what is the meaning behind difficult verses) in a brief easy-to-read format. The column has been a great success. A year after the column began I was privileged to win the 2015 *Catholic Press Association Award* for "Best Regular Column: Scripture" and the column is still going strong today.

Over the last few years, requests started to come in from readers asking for these columns to be collected and published for easy reference. This book, *Behind the Bible: What the Bible Assumes You Already Know* is my answer to these requests. Since variety is the spice of life, my articles didn't follow any particular order. It jumped around from the Old Testament and the New Testament sometimes zeroing in on the biblical background of one particular verse and other times zooming out to look at the Bible as a whole. For the reader's convenience, the subjects have been placed in the order of the books of the Bible. That way, if you are working through the Bible book by book, this group of essays will follow along with your reading. For those who wish to follow the publication date, a date is also supplies in each title.

My hope was to encourage my readers to dig in deep into Scripture, so much of what is said in these articles is given only an appetizer. There is often much more that can be said on the subject. For those who'd like more in-depth explanations of some of the subjects touched on, I would suggest looking up the Catholic Production's page www.GaryMichuta.com. There you'll find my books and CDs that go into several of these topics in more depth.

Also, you can access these articles and the most recent installments to the series at the Michigan Catholic Newspaper website at: http://www.themichigancatholic.org

Thanks and I hope that you enjoy reading this book!

OLD TESTAMENT

A Brief Look at Biblical Time (October 27, 2016)

Unlike our previous articles that focused on the background of a particular Scripture text, this installment is going to look at the idea of biblical time. Why spend time talking about time?

Well, the Bible is sacred history, and if you've read a lot of Scripture, you've probably noticed how different events often seem eerily similar. It's almost as though Scripture's view of time is a little different than our own.

This idea of "biblical time" is perhaps best explained by comparing and contrasting the pagan and modern views of time.

The pagans understood time to be cyclical. According to this view, everything that *has* happened will happen again and again into eternity. For most of us, this worldview isn't very appealing; after all, if everything repeats, then everything is fated to happen and there is nothing you can do to prevent it. It's not surprising, therefore, that the pagans generally denied the existence of free will. For them, we are all just pawns in an endless circle of life.

The modern view of time, on the other hand, is as a straight line of events, one linked to the other by a series of causes, never to be repeated. While current events may shape future events, ultimately the road ahead is open to possibilities. While this worldview does break us out of the pagan prison of repeating cycles, the drawback is that this view might see two distant events in history as completely unrelated.

This forgets, however, that God also acts in history. Indeed, he is the Lord of history. Although two distant historical events might seem totally unrelated to us, they *are* related in God's providence. Because Sacred Scripture unveils the religious meaning of history, it gives us a deeper perspective on how events might relate to each other.

Biblical time is neither an unbreakable cycle, like the pagans believed, nor a straight line like we see things today. Rather, time unfolds in Scripture much like an ascending spiral. For example, while Moses' exodus out of Egypt was a one-time event, the pattern of the exodus does seem to repeat itself in different and more spiritually revealing ways, culminating with Jesus, the New Moses, establishing a new Passover (the Mass) and freeing us from the slavery of sin and leading us into the new Promised Land, heaven. Moses and Jesus are two different persons, but both events are related.

We saw another example of this "unfolding spiral" in an earlier installment of "Behind the Bible," which examined how Noah's flood and its aftermath are described in Scripture using elements from the Creation narrative in Genesis 1-2. Although the creation of cosmos and Noah's flood are two entirely distinct events, nevertheless, Scripture sees Noah's flood as an echo of what occurred in the first chapters of Genesis.

The spiral view of sacred history is of great benefit to us today. It makes the sacred past applicable to how we ought to live today. For example, Paul teaches that Moses and the people during the exodus also underwent a kind of baptism and ate spiritual food, yet nevertheless disobeyed God and died in the desert. Such things are not relics of the past, but, as he says, they are examples for us and for our instruction (1 Corinthians 10:1-12).

Sacred history also gives us great confidence in God's mercy. From it we learn that in whatever situation we find ourselves, God is faithful. As Sirach 2:8-9 says, "Study the generations long past and understand; has anyone hoped in the LORD and been disappointed? Has anyone persevered in his fear and been forsaken? Has anyone called upon him and been rebuffed?"

Why Did the Authors of the Bible Cite Non-biblical Sources? (June 10, 2016)

While we commonly think of the Bible as "a book," it really isn't. The Bible is probably best described as a book of books or even a library. It contains 73 books composed by different human authors and written at different times, places and occasions.

The Bible is like a library in another respect, too. It contains not only books, but also information about other books. The Old Testament, for example, mentions a number of works that no longer exist. These books are not Scripture, but they were writings that the authors either knew or consulted when they were writing their inspired manuscript.

Why would the inspired authors of Scripture need to consult books? Weren't they inspired? Sometimes we incorrectly think of inspiration as the Holy Spirit overcoming the sacred author's body and forcing them to write things about they had no knowledge or control, like the pagan oracles of old. Such was not the case.

God is much greater than that. He doesn't have to wrestle against what He created or mug the intellect of an author to compose Scripture. God is so powerful that He can work through the secondary human author's abilities, knowledge and personality in a way that doesn't overcome their freedom.

As the Vatican II document on Divine Revelation ("Dei Verbum") explains, "In composing the sacred books, God chose men and while employed by Him they made use of their powers and abilities, so that with Him acting in them and through them, they, as true authors, consigned to writing everything and only those things which He wanted."

Because the secondary human authors of Scripture are "true authors" and "made use of their power and abilities" when they wrote their respective books of Scripture, they still needed to acquire knowledge about what they wrote. Therefore, they consulted other works. The following is a list of works mentioned in the Old Testament.

- The Book of Jasher (Joshua 10:13, 2 Samuel 1:18)
- The Book of the Wars of the Lord (Numbers 21:14)
- The Chronicles of the Kings of Israel (1 Kings 14:19)
- The Chronicles of the Kings of Judah (1 Kings 14:29)
- The Chronicles of Solomon (1 Kings 11:41)
- The Chronicles of King David (1 Chronicles 27:24)
- The History of Samuel the Seer and the History of Gad the Seer (1 Chronicles 29:29)

- The Book of Shemaiah (2 Chronicles 9:29; 12:15; 13:22)
- The Midrash of the Book of Kings (2 Chronicles 24:27)
- The Chronicles of the Kings of Israel (2 Chronicles 33:18)
- The History of the Seers (2 Chronicles 33:19)
- The Annals of King Ahasuerus (Ester 2:23; 6:1; 10:2)
- The Book of Chronicles (Nehemiah 12:23)
- Nehemiah's Memoirs (2 Maccabees 2:13)
- The Five books of Jason of Cyrene (2 Maccabees 2:23)

As you can see, these texts all involve history. We tend to think that because the Bible is the only ancient source to survive antiquity that speaks to certain events, it must have been the only writing to ever write about them. This list tells a different story. There were plenty of books, histories, annals and other records in circulation at the time the books of the Bible were written. The Old Testament authors were familiar with them. Not only that, but the biblical authors even direct their original readers to these works for reference.

This is comforting because it shows how deeply rooted the Old Testament is in history. It wasn't an isolated author reporting what happened; there were plenty of non-inspired writings that also recorded the events of the time. It's nice to know that even the inspired authors weren't immune from doing research and citing sources.

Genesis 1 - 2 (Wisdom 11:18): The "First Creation" and the "Second Creation": An Often Forgotten Distinction (April 25, 2017)

One of the last Old Testament books to be written is a book called The Wisdom of Solomon, or Wisdom for short. It is one of only two Old Testament books known to be originally composed in Greek, rather than Hebrew or Aramaic. In many ways, Wisdom is one of the most beautiful books to read.

Unfortunately, it is also one book that has been unfairly maligned by some. It is one of the seven Old Testament deuterocanonical books that have been rejected by Protestants as uninspired, or what they call the "Apocrypha." In fact, most Protestant Bibles exclude this book altogether.

Wisdom also has raised a few eyebrows because it, unlike any other Old Testament work, seems to use terms and ideas that come from Greek philosophy. As a result, not a few non-Catholics have accused Wisdom of being "too Greek" to the point of being in error. In their haste to dismiss this book from the rolls of inspired literature, they've raised charges against certain passages that they believe contradict Judeo-Christian revelation. One such passage is Wisdom 11:18, which reads:

"For not without means was your almighty hand, that had fashioned the universe from formless matter…"

From this passage, people have rashly charged that the author has embraced Greek philosophy because the ancient Greeks believed that the universe (matter) was eternal, unlike the Christian doctrine that teaches that God created all things from nothing (Latin, *ex nihilo*). According to these critics, Wisdom 11:18 denies creation from nothing, opting for the Greek notion that God merely fashioned the universe from formless pre-existing matter. Wisdom, therefore, cannot be Scripture!

Does Wisdom 11:18 really reject creation from nothing? Not at all. The reason it might seem to many to be doing so is because we've forgotten about a very important and fascinating biblical distinction found in Genesis 1 that was recognized by the early Church fathers. This distinction concerns what the early fathers called the "first creation" (Latin, *creatio prima*) and the "second creation" (*creatio secondo*).

You might have noticed that the creation narrative in the first chapter of Genesis begins in a very odd way. It reads, "In the beginning, when God created the heavens and the earth…" (Genesis 1:1). It then continues by describing how God turns the formless and void earth and brings about land, water, sky, animals, etc. As the early Church father Severian of Gabala (d. AD 408) wrote:

> "On the first day God created out of nothing whatever He has made; but on the following days He did not create out of nothing, but according to His good pleasure fashioned that which He had made on the first day."

But when does God create all things from nothing? It occurs in Genesis 1:1, "In the beginning, when God created the heavens and the earth…" This is the first creation (*creatio prima*) or creation proper. As Severian of Gabala notes, everything that came afterward was fashioned from what was made on the first day. This is what is called the "second creation" (*creatio secondo*).

Severian was not the only early Church father to notice this distinction. The three great Cappadocian fathers recognized it, along with St. Augustine. As to whether God immediately followed creation from nothing with fashioning what he made is an open question. Genesis doesn't tell us, although the early fathers generally believed that there was an interval between creation proper and God's work of separation and forming.

Keeping this view in mind, let's look again at Wisdom 11:18. Because many people have forgotten the distinction between the first and second creation, they assume any writing referring to creation must be speaking about God creating all things from nothing. However, this is not the case. Wisdom 11:18 is not speaking about the first creation (creation from nothing), but the second creation in which God fashions what He has made.

In other words, Wisdom 11:17 is not denying Genesis 1:1 — God created the heavens and the earth — but it is commenting on what God did from Genesis 1:2 onward. Wisdom 11:17 didn't replace Jewish-Christian revelation with Greek philosophy; rather, it is revealing an important distinction that many often miss.

Genesis 3:7 - Adam and the Fig Leaf: An Uncomfortable Wardrobe Choice (June 26, 2015)

We're all familiar with the story of the fall of Adam and Eve; how they followed the temptation of the Serpent and ate the fruit. As a result, Genesis 3:7 says, "Then the eyes of both of them were opened, and they realized that they were naked; so they sewed fig leaves together and made loincloths for themselves." And you know the rest of the story. But did you ever wonder why our first parents chose to make garments of fig leafs?

The first reason was so that they could hide their nakedness before God. The early Church fathers saw that Adam and Eve's disobedience to God was a type of spiritual adultery, and because Original Sin is passed down through natural generation, they wanted to cover these areas of the body in shame. But why fig leafs?

Were fig leaves were the first thing they could find that could be sewn into clothing? Possibly. But there might be a second reason that has escaped our notice. We don't live in a part of the world where fig trees commonly grow. According to Balfour's *Plants in the Bible,* "The (fig) tree is a native of the East, and has been transported into Europe. It is grown in the south of Europe, including Greece and Italy; and in Northern and Western Africa. A wild type is known in Italy by the name of Caprifico." You normally don't see fig trees growing in the northern Midwest, so chances are you don't know much about them.

Fig trees are not very user-friendly. They contain an enzyme call "ficin," which, when touched, can cause severe skin irritation. If you'd like to see how gruesome fig tree rashes can get, jump on your favorite search engine and type "fig tree rash." Trust me. These rashes are not pretty.

What's fascinating is that our first parents, after they had sinned, decided to cover themselves with these itchy, irritating leaves. Why?

The early Church fathers, who knew fig trees very well, saw that this new clothing had some spiritual significance. For example, St. Augustine understood these itchy coverings to signify the "irritations of lust to which he had been reduced by sinning." In other words, just as these leaves cause irritation to force us to scratch, they signify how the irritation of lust beckons us to sin.

Another, similar way to look at the fig leaf clothes is to see them as penitential garb. It has long been a custom within the Church for those who are called to such acts to wear clothing that is uncomfortable as an act of penance. For example, Scripture speaks of people being clothed in sackcloth (Genesis 37:34, 2 Samuel 3:31, and Esther 4:1). This rough clothing is uncomfortable and itchy. It's possible that Adam and Eve didn't make their first clothes out of fig leaves by accident; they may have not only wished to cover their nakedness, but to repent of what they did.

In Genesis 3:21, God gives Adam and Eve a new pair of clothes: animal skins. These skins may not have been quite as bad as the fig leaves, but according to St. Ambrose, these animal skins were penitential as well: "God cast Adam out of Paradise immediately after his fault; there was no delay. At once the fallen were severed from all their enjoyments that they might do penance; at once God clothed them with garments of skins, not of silk."

It's amazing how a little detail like fig leaves can add another level of meaning to a familiar story. It just goes to show that there is often a reward for those who are willing to dig a little "Behind the Bible."

Genesis 6:5, 12 - Noah, the Flood, and Creation in Reverse (September 30, 2016)

Most of us are familiar with the story of Noah's flood, but did you know that Scripture describes Noah's flood in ways that harken back to the creation story? This suggestion might seem strange at first, but there are some uncanny parallels. Let's examine a few.

When God created the heavens and the earth, He said after each day, "It is good." He finishes creation on the sixth day, when he says again, "It is very good" (Genesis 1:31). The flood story, however, begins with God's stating His disapproval. He looked upon earth and saw that everyone except Noah and his family were wicked (Genesis 6:5, 12). Creation is completed with divine approval, and the destruction of the world begins with divine disapproval.

The next two parallels concern water. What does water have to do with creation? You might have missed it, but it's there. Before the first day of creation, "The earth was without form and void, and darkness was upon the face of the deep; and the Spirit of God was moving over the face of the waters" (Genesis 1:2). As 2 Peter 3:5 explains, "… the earth was formed out of water and through water by the word of God." Water preceded the creation of the plants, animals and humans, and with Noah's flood the process is reversed; plants, animals and humans were destroyed by water.

Even the flood itself harkens back to creation. We often think that 40 days and nights of rain caused the flood, but that's not how the Bible describes it. Genesis 7:11 says, "All the fountains of the great abyss burst forth, and the floodgates of the sky were opened." The flood waters came from the sky and the ground! That's strange. Why would water come from the ground? Look at the second day of creation. On the second day, God separated the "waters above" from the "water below" (Genesis 1:6-8). The flood reverses what God had accomplished on the second day of creation so that these two bodies of water were no longer separated.

Day four of creation is also present in Noah's flood. On the fourth day, God created the sun and moon to "…mark the fixed times, the days and the years." The flood temporarily suspended these seasons, so that after the flood God promised, "As long as the earth lasts, seedtime and harvest, cold and heat, summer and winter, and day and night shall not cease" (Genesis 8:22).

Even the seven days of creation as a whole finds its place within the flood narrative. God created the heavens and the earth and completed filling the earth with plants, animals and humans in a six-day period and rested on the seventh day. In Genesis 7:4, we learn that God commanded Noah to gather all the animals and his family into the ark within seven days. After seven days, the flood begins and the world returns to a watery chaos.

The parallels with creation continue even after flood. For example, Genesis 8:1 says that "…God remembered Noah … and caused a wind to pass over the earth, and the water subsided." The same Hebrew word translated "wind" is also translated as "spirit" in Genesis 1:2 (i.e., "the Spirit of God was moving over the face of the waters"). Creation begins with the spirit over the water and Noah's flood ends with the spirit or wind moving over the water.

There are even some parallels between Noah and Adam. Genesis 2:7 tells us that God created Adam from the earth. In Hebrew, there is a word play between the word "Adam" and the word for earth (*adamah*). Strangely enough, Noah is described as a "man of the earth" (*ish ha-adamah*) in Genesis 9:20. Noah, like Adam, was commanded by God to be "fruitful and multiply" (Genesis 9:1, 7). Moreover, Adam was righteous, sinned and was cursed (Genesis 3:17-18). Similarly, Noah was a righteous man, who sins (Genesis 9:20-21) and his sin is followed by a curse (Genesis 9:20-25).

The next time you read Noah's flood, take some time and look for these and other parallels with the creation narrative. You might be surprised at what you'll find.

Genesis 9:3-5 - Why Did the Old Covenant Forbid Blood? (July 25, 2014)

There are many precepts in the Old Covenant that seem strange to our modern ears. For example, the Old Covenant had a prohibition of drinking blood or eating flesh with blood in it. How odd that God would forbid such a thing! Why would God be concerned about drinking blood?

To answer this, we must dig a little deeper into Scripture. The earliest command not to drink blood comes from the time of Noah. God said, "Every creature that is alive shall be yours to eat; I give them all to you as I did the green plants. Only flesh with its lifeblood still in it you shall not eat. For your own lifeblood, too, I will demand an accounting: from every animal I will demand it, and from man in regard to his fellow man I will demand an accounting for human life" (Gen 9:3-5).

The ancients associated blood with life. After all, if an animal loses its blood, it dies. This association between blood and life can also be seen in Leviticus, where God says: "Since the life of every living body is its blood, I have told the Israelites: You shall not partake of the blood of any meat. Since the life of every living body is its blood, anyone who partakes of it shall be cut off" (Deut 12:23).

Carrying this association further, one can see how drinking blood or eating meat with blood would signify a communication or participation in the victim's life. This appears to be the logic that lies behind many pagan sacrifices and rituals. By drinking the blood of an ox, for example, the person gains the power or strength of the ox. What's worse, pagans often worshiped animal gods. So drinking the blood of animals or eating meat with blood in it was not so innocent. It was an attempt to enter into communion with these gods.

You can see why God would be concerned about this practice. Indeed, the Old Testament instructions against drinking blood often appear alongside other prohibitions against idolatrous practices, such a divinization (e.g., Leviticus 17:7-10, 19:26-28, et. al.). By stigmatizing the drinking of blood, God made this form of idolatry less attractive.

This brings up another question: If God forbade the drinking of blood in the Old Testament, why are we permitted to partake of the Eucharistic Body and Blood in the New Testament? Wouldn't this be a contradiction?

There are several reasons why not. Here are three.

• First, the prohibition of drinking blood was part of the Old Covenant ceremonial law. The ceremonial law was given to order Old Covenant worship of the one true God, to train the people of God for the coming of the Messiah (Gal 3:23-26), and to foreshadow Christ (Col 2:16-17). Once the Messiah has come, however, the ceremonial law became obsolete (Gal 3:25, Col 3:24-25, Heb 8:13).

• Second, Christ is God. Therefore, he has the authority to propose a new law that supersedes the old (Matt 5:27-48, 11:29, 28:18; 1 Cor 9:21; Gal 6:2; James 2:8). The New Law commands us to partake of Christ's Body and Blood (John 6:53-56). Therefore, Christ's command makes it permissible.

• Third, the prohibition against drinking blood seems to be tied to the practice of pagans who attempted to share in the life of animals or demons (1 Cor 10:19-21). This is, of course, wrong. It's idolatry.

However, the opposite is true in regard to sharing in the life of God. Sharing in the life of God is an act of true worship that is both desirable and necessary (John 6:57, 11:25, 14:6, 15:4-5; 1 John 5:11-12; 2 Peter 1:4). Our life is in Christ and "Life in Christ has its foundation in the Eucharistic banquet: 'As the living Father sent me, and I live because of the Father, so he who eats me will live because of me'" (CCC 1391, John 6:57).

As you can see, it is sometimes the most unusual things in Scripture, like prohibiting the drinking of blood, that offer interesting insights into the past and can even point to profound truths.

Exodus

Exodus 3:7-8 - Why the 10 Plagues on Egypt? (August 18, 2016)

One of the most pivotal events in salvation history is the exodus from Egypt. The Israelites were trapped in the bondage of slavery in Egypt when God called Moses to free them. God said to Moses, "…'I have witnessed the affliction of my people in Egypt and have heard their cry of complaint against their slave drivers, so I know well what they are suffering. Therefore I have come down to rescue them … and lead them out of that land into a good and spacious land …" (Exodus 3:7-8).

What's fascinating about God's emancipation of the Israelites is the way He went about it. God could have sent Moses to Pharaoh with the message "Let my people go," performed one astounding miracle, and the Israelites would have been freed to go to the Promised Land. But He didn't. Instead, God choose to do it through 10 plagues. Why? Because the bondage that the Israelites experienced in Egypt went beyond physical servitude; they were in spiritual slavery, too. Therefore, the Israelites needed to escape not just Egypt, but its idolatry as well.

For this reason, God did not immediately say to Pharaoh, "Let my people go." Instead, God's first command was to allow the Israelites to make a three-day journey into the desert to offer sacrifice (Exodus 3:18). Why did the Israelites need to offer sacrifices in the desert and not in Egypt? Because they were going to repudiate the gods of Egypt by sacrificing the very animals the Egyptians worshipped. Had the Israelites sacrificed these animals in a city, they would have been stoned (Exodus 8:22). Therefore, the first step in the exodus was to free the Israelites of idolatry.

Knowing that Pharaoh would refuse this command, God offered these sacrifices Himself symbolically through the 10 plagues, with each of the plagues corresponding to an Egyptian god. For example, the first plague turned the water into blood. This plague appears to be aimed at the Egyptian god of the Nile, Hapi. The plague of frogs corresponds to the goddess Haket, who was depicted as a frog.

The third and fourth plagues of gnats and flies are a little more difficult to identify. They may have been aimed at Uatchit, a god depicted as an Ichneuman fly, or one of several other deities. The fifth plague, the death of livestock, corresponds to Apis, the bull god, and Hathor, a cow-headed goddess of the deserts. The plague of boils and sores showed the powerlessness of Shekhmet, goddess of healing, or perhaps Thoth, a god associated with science and medicine. Hail aimed at the sky god, Nut.

The eighth plague was the invasion of locusts. This was a judgment on Senahem, a locust-headed god. The ninth plague was three days of darkness; the Egyptians had several gods of sun and light, such as Re, Aten and Atum. The final plague, the death of the first-born sons, would show the powerlessness of Osiris, the god of life and patron of Pharaoh.

The 10 plagues of Egypt, therefore, were not simply a show of force, a game of "Can you top this?" Rather, they were judgments upon the idolatry of the Egyptians (Numbers 33:4) in which God manifested to all that these false gods are nothing compared to the true and living God.

One would think that after seeing what God had done to these false gods that the Israelites would never shrink back to their former way of life, but such was not the case. There's a saying, "You can take a boy out of the country, but you can't take the country of out the boy." The same is true for the Israelites. Later in Exodus, the Israelites worshipped a golden calf that they made in the form of the Egyptian fertility god Apis, saying, "This is your God, O Israel, who brought you out of the land of Egypt" (Exodus 32:4). Even though the Israelites were freed from physical bondage, they still were in spiritual bondage.

The rest of the Old Testament chronicles their spiritual emancipation, culminating in the arrival of a new Moses, who institutes a new Passover, and opens the way to our true promise land in heaven, Jesus the Messiah.

Exodus 15:26 - The Healing "Code" of the Earliest Christians (October 20, 2015)

I'm always fascinated by leads that shed light on early Church history, especially those that illuminate areas of history we know little about. One such lead comes from Exodus 15:26.

After traveling in the desert for three days with nothing to drink, Moses comes upon a pool of water at Marah. However, the water at Marah was bitter. The people complained and Moses sought the Lord's help. God told Moses to throw a certain piece of wood into the water and the water became sweet. God then said to Moses:

"'If you really listen to the voice of the LORD, your God ... and do what is right in his eyes: if you heed his commandments and keep all his precepts, I will not afflict you with any of the diseases with which I afflicted the Egyptians; for I, the LORD, am your healer'" (Exodus 15:26).

The early Church fathers saw the wood as a foreshadowing of the cross, which sweetened the bitterness of the Law of Moses.

In itself, this passage is interesting, but once it is combined with two other elements it becomes illuminating.

The first element has to do with numbers. Hebrew, like many other ancient languages, didn't use numbers. Instead, they used letters for numbers, as with Roman numerals where each letter has a value ("I" = one; "V" = five; "X" = 10 and so on). To write a number, one only has to combine different letters. An interesting off-shoot of this is that words have numerical values. For example, Jesus' name "Yeshua" has a numerical value of 391. This will become important later.

The second element is healing in the early Church. Anyone familiar with the Acts of the Apostles knows that miraculous healings were abundant in the early Church, which occurred with the invocation of the holy name of Jesus (Acts 4:30). Now, we know this happened in Acts, but what happened afterward? Did it continue?

Curiously enough, a few early rabbinical writings address this phenomenon of healing. For example, one story relates how rabbi Eleazar ben Damah was bitten by a snake and a man named Jacob came to heal him in "...the name of Jesus son of Pantera." But Jacob was prevented from coming to ben Damah and he died. The story ends with a blessing of ben Damah for dying in peace without transgressing the "hedge erected by the sages" (Tosefta-tractate Hullin 2:22-4 2:23). The "hedge erected by the sages" appears to be an effort by the rabbis to stop Christians from healing in Jesus' name.

The final piece of this puzzle comes from another rabbinical work that involves Exodus 15:26. It is a short and simple condemnation:

> "R. Akiba adds: He who reads the external books; and he who whispers over a wound, saying: All the sickness which I brought on Egypt I will not bring upon thee, etc. (Exodus 15:26). Abba Saul adds: He who pronounces the Name with its proper letters" (Tosefta Sanhedrin XII, 10).

It's clear that Akiba ban is referencing Christians healing in the name of Jesus. But why didn't the early Christians whisper the name of Jesus over the wound? Why quote Exodus 15:26 instead?

Noted Jewish scholar Louis Ginzberg proposes that the answer lies in the last words of the verse: "I YHWH (Yahweh) am your healer." The numerical value of these words comes out to 391; the same numerical value as the name Jesus.

When we put all the pieces of the puzzle together, we can trace out what happens after Acts. It appears that certain measures were taken to stem the tide of healings and conversions to Christianity. At first, the use of the name "Jesus" was forbidden. So our forefathers did the next best thing: they whispered Exodus 15:26 over a wound, which had the same numerical value as the name Jesus. God honored this and continued to work miracles, until, eventually, whispering of Exodus 15:26 was banned as well. This is such a great example of our early fathers being "shrewd as serpents and simple as doves" in their efforts to make Jesus better known and loved.

Exodus 34:29-30 - Unveiling Moses (June 30, 2017)

A rather peculiar thing happened to Moses while he was on Mount Sinai receiving the law. Scripture says: "As Moses came down from Mount Sinai with the two tablets of the commandments in his hands, he did not know that the skin of his face had become radiant while he conversed with the LORD. When Aaron, then, and the other Israelites saw Moses and noticed how radiant the skin of his face had become, they were afraid to come near him...." (Exodus 34:29-30).

So different was Moses' appearance that Aaron and the people were afraid to come near him. Moses then began an interesting ritual. Moses put on a veil when speaking to the people.

As Exodus 34:34-35 tells us:

> "Whenever Moses entered the presence of the LORD to converse with him, he removed the veil until he came out again. On coming out, he would tell the Israelites all that had been commanded. Then the Israelites would see that the skin of Moses' face was radiant; so he would again put the veil over his face until he went in to converse with the LORD."

There are a few interesting side notes about this episode. The Hebrew text describes the brilliant radiance of Moses using the word *qeren*, a word that is used elsewhere in the Old Testament for the horns of an animal (e.g., Psalm 69:32). When St. Jerome encountered this word, he translated it into Latin as "horns," so that Exodus 34:29 reads: "And when Moses came down from the Mount Sinai, he held the two tables of the testimony, and he knew not that his face was horned from the conversation of the Lord." St. Jerome wasn't alone. An ancient Jewish translation called Aquila also translated it "horned." Jerome's translation is the reason why sometimes in Christian art Moses is depicted with horns on his head, as is the case with Michelangelo's Moses. What the Hebrew was trying to express was that Moses' face emitted beams of light.

Another interesting feature is that whenever Moses "turned to the Lord," he would take off his veil, but when he turned away from the Lord to speak to the people he would put the veil back on. Both St. Paul and the early Church fathers saw this action as significant. In 2 Corinthians 3:12-16, Paul says:

> "Therefore, since we have such hope, we act very boldly and not like Moses, who put a veil over his face so that the Israelites could not look intently at the cessation of what was fading."

Where God revealed his Law through Moses, who was veiled, the ministers of Christ speak boldly and without a veil so that God's glory would be fully revealed.

Paul likewise saw Moses' instruction of the people while wearing a veil as a sign that the fulfillment of the Law was partially obscured. Paul continues:

"Rather, their thoughts were rendered dull, for to this present day the same veil remains unlifted when they read the old covenant, because through Christ it is taken away. To this day, in fact, whenever Moses is read, a veil lies over their hearts, but whenever a person turns to the Lord the veil is removed."

We can relate to Paul's point. There is an old saying: Hindsight is 20/20. It's always easier to see things more clearly in the past than in the present. Before the messiah came, the prophecies about him and the New Covenant were difficult to make out. However, once Christ did come and gave the Holy Spirit to his disciples, the obscure things in the Law became recognizable as if a veil had been removed.

This episode with Moses also teaches us one more thing: Encountering God transforms a person. Moses physically was changed after his encounter with the Lord. Likewise, we, too, are changed when we draw closer to God and know him more. We become more like him and we are transformed into his image (2 Corinthians 3:18). When Moses returned to the people, they immediately noticed that he was different. If you consider yourself close to God, do people notice that you're different?

Deuteronomy

Deuteronomy 28:66 - The Cross and the Old Testament (February 23, 2017)

The most horrific method of execution in the ancient Roman world was crucifixion. It was a method that was so horrible that the most refined Romans wouldn't even mention it by name. The cross was also a stumbling block for non-believing Jews, as it seemed absurd that the Messiah would come and die in such an ignoble fashion. Christians, however, revere the cross because it is through Christ's suffering and death that he offered a perfect sacrifice for sin. Through their diligent and prayerful study of Scripture, the early Church fathers discovered several passages that they believed hinted or even foretold that Christ would be crucified. Let's look at some of the most interesting passages.

St. Cyril of Jerusalem, St. Athanasius, and others believed that Deuteronomy 28:66 (LXX) alluded to the crucifixion when it said, "And thy life shall hang before your eyes; thou shalt fear night and day, neither shalt thou trust thy life.'" This verse is found among the covenant curses that fell upon those who broke God's covenant with Moses. Essentially, it means "your life is in the balance." Knowing that Christ is the Way, the Truth, and the Life (John 14:6-7), several early Church fathers saw "…thy life shall hang before your eyes," as an obscure allusion to Christ our life being hung on the cross.

The fathers also saw another cryptic from the prophet Jeremiah. Just as the life of David is in some ways mirrored in the life of Christ, so too the suffering of Jeremiah. During one such passage, where Jeremiah reflects upon those who persecute him, he writes, "Yet I, like a trusting lamb led to slaughter, had not realized that they were hatching plots against me: 'Let us destroy the tree in its vigor; let us cut him off from the land of the living, so that his name will be spoken no more'" (Jeremiah 10:19). In the ancient Greek translation of the Old Testament, called the Septuagint (or LXX), the line "Let us destroy the tree and its vigor" is translated as "Let us put wood upon his bread…" Since Christ, at the Last Supper took bread and said, "This is my body," the early fathers understood this passage to mean, "Let us put the wood of the cross upon Christ's body" therefore alluding to the crucifixion.

The crucifixion was also foreshadowed in the Old Testament as types. For example, Moses mounted a serpent on a pole so that whoever would look upon it would be healed (Numbers 21:9). Christ points to this as a type of his own crucifixion (John 3:13). Noah's ark was also a type of the cross since it was through the wood of the ark that Noah and his family were saved. Another type of the saving power of the cross is found in Exodus 15:25-26. In this passage, the Israelites encounter the water at Marah, which was too bitter to drink. Moses placed a piece of wood into the water and it was made fresh and sweet so that the Israelites could drink it.

In addition to references to wood, the early fathers also saw references to the wounds of Christ. In Psalms 22:17-19 (LXX), it says "…they pierced my hands and my feet. They counted all my bones; and they observed and looked upon me. They parted my garments among themselves, and cast lots upon my raiment." Likewise, Zechariah 12:10 says, "…they shall look upon him whom they have pierced."

Some early fathers also saw the outstretched arms of Jesus on the cross being foretold as an plea to the wicked, as in Isaiah 65:2 where God said, "I have stretched out my hands all the day to a rebellious people, who walk in evil paths and follow their own thoughts…," and as a sacrificial act, as when Psalm 141:2 says, "Let my prayer be counted as incense before you, and the lifting up of my hands as an evening sacrifice!"

These prophecies of the cross vary in strength, but all of them may be helpful for fruitful mediation and prayer on the crucifixion, especially during the upcoming Lenten season.

Esther

Esther's Rocky Journey to the Bible (Feb. 5, 2015)

Quick! Name the first Old Testament book that comes to mind. Isaiah? Psalms? Genesis? I can almost guarantee Esther wasn't among the first. Why not? Well, probably because it's smaller or it might seem less interesting than the others. But don't let its size fool you. The book of Esther, like its heroine, is a fighter, and in this installment of "Behind the Bible," we are going to look at this little book's rocky journey to join the canon of Scripture.

The book of Esther tells the story of the Jews who remained in exile after the Babylonian captivity had ended. Esther had become queen, and a high official named Haman was demanding that his subjects bow down to him in homage. A righteous man named Mordecai refused to bow down, and caught wind of Haman's plot to kill all the Jews in the Kingdom.

Mordecai appealed to Esther to intercede with the king on behalf of the Jewish people. Because Esther did so, the king turned against Haman, executing him on the same gallows on which he planned to execute the Jews.

Just like its heroine, the book of Esther had to overcome formidable opposition as well. Our story begins with the book itself. There are two versions of Esther: a longer and a shorter version. The longer version contains six sections (A-F) in Greek that include prayers, acts of piety, a letter, and other details. The shorter Hebrew version excludes these sections, reducing the story of Esther to almost a secular account. Indeed, the shorter Hebrew version of Esther never even mentions the name of God!

The earliest Christians and the Church have always accepted the longer version of Esther. In fact, one of the earliest non-biblical Christian writings we possess, 1 Clement, written at the end of the first century or the beginning of the second, commends Esther to its readers, speaking of her fasting and prayer, which is only found in the longer version (1 Clement 55). Likewise, around the same time, the Jewish historian Josephus also used the longer version of Esther in his book "Antiquities of the Jews" (Antiquities 11, 6).

Long Live the Queen

Troubles for the book of Esther started sometime between A.D. 100-135, when the Rabbinical Bible was formed. By adopting a single Hebrew text as their biblical norm, the rabbis naturally opted for the shorter Hebrew version of Esther. But we know this inclusion was not without opposition. Some rabbis continued to dispute Esther's sacred status. In fact, several early Church fathers composed lists of the book of the Old Testament accepted in rabbinical Judaism, and some of these lists either omit Esther or note that it was disputed. It wasn't until the late fourth century that Esther seems to be universally accepted in Judaism. Ironically, it's also around this time that troubles began brewing in the Church.

Pope Damasus I commissioned St. Jerome to make a fresh Latin translation of the Bible. But Jerome decided to translate the Old Testament not from the Greek Septuagint, as others have done, but from the same Hebrew text the rabbis adopted in the second century A.D. And as you may have guessed, he had a problem with Esther. Incorrectly believing this Hebrew text was identical to the inspired original, Jerome rejected the Greek sections of Esther as "Apocrypha" — that is, non-inspired additions. The Church reaffirmed the historic Christian canon against Jerome, but Esther's troubles didn't end there.

In the 1600s, when Protestants rejected certain Catholic doctrines as unbiblical, Catholics responded by appealing to Scripture, which included the Deuterocanon (i.e., Tobit, Judith, Baruch, Wisdom, Sirach, 1 and 2 Maccabees, and the longer versions of Esther and Daniel). Protestants in turn appealed to St. Jerome, and accepted only the books found in the Rabbinical Bible. As a result, Protestant Bibles today use the shorter, more secular, version of Esther rather than the longer version used by the Church.

Which only goes to show that even the most humble and inconspicuous books contain fascinating stories when you look Behind the Bible.

THE PROPHETS

Ezekiel 1:1 - Spinning Ezekiel's wheels (October 14, 2016)

Beyond a doubt, the first chapter of Ezekiel is one of the strangest chapters in Scripture. God appears to the prophet on top of a magnificent throne in order to commission him to prophesy to Israel. What is strange about this appearance is how the prophet describes God's throne. God is seated above a firmament held aloft by four strange living creatures and wheels within wheels. Ezekiel's detailed description of each of these elements was so strange and mysterious that young rabbis were forbidden from studying this chapter apparently out of fear that it might lead to unadvised speculation.

This rabbinical prohibition was wise. I remember as a young boy picking up a book that claimed that what Ezekiel was describing wasn't God's magnificent throne at all, but an ancient wheel-like U.F.O. That's right, a U.F.O.! But there is a better and more authentic way to understand this ancient symbolic language than resorting to alien spaceships.

The problem with the book was that it failed to understand the ancient use of symbolism. The author of the U.F.O. book thought Ezekiel's description was a primitive literal description of an alien spacecraft when what he was really trying to express was certain qualities or abilities of the angels. We know this because later in

Ezekiel 10:20, the prophet tells us that the four living creatures were Cherubim.

But you have to give the book some credit. Ezekiel's description is very unusual: "…their form was human, but each had four faces and four wings, and their legs went straight down; the soles of their feet were round. They sparkled with a gleam like burnished bronze. Their faces were like this: each of the four had the face of a man, but on the right side was the face of a lion, and on the left side the face of an ox, and finally each had the face of an eagle" (Ezekiel 1:5-7, 10).

If Ezekiel was describing angels, why did he give such a strange description of them? Didn't he know that angels don't have bodies? Of course he did. His description uses common physical things to point us to the immaterial traits of these magnificent angelic creatures. For example, Ezekiel describes the four faces on each living creature as being that of a man, a lion, an ox and an eagle. Each of these faces points to a special trait that each Cherubim possesses. The human face denotes intellect or reason. The lion's face denotes majesty. The ox denotes strength and the eagle denotes speed or agility. All these traits were present in each of the four Cherubim.

Perhaps the strangest description of all is Ezekiel's vision of the four wheels within wheels:

> "The wheels … were constructed as though one wheel were within another. They could move in any of the four directions they faced, without veering as they moved. The four of them had rims,

and I saw that their rims were full of eyes all around" (Ezekiel 1:16-18).

The ancient rabbis understood these wheels to be another type of angel known as the Serafim. This might seem odd at first, but if Ezekiel's descriptions point to traits, then Ezekiel's wheels are just another way of describing the traits of these Serafim. His description suggests that there were two wheels in each set facing at a 90-degree angle, so that it can move in any direction without turning. (Don't try to imagine it, you'll get a headache.) What Ezekiel wished to convey was that these angels had unrestricted and effortless mobility. As for their rims being "full of eyes all around," the image suggests that the mobility of the Serafim was complimented by being able to see or understand all that is around them.

Because we are so used to literal descriptions, Ezekiel's portrait might seem bizarre, but there is a certain beauty behind his method. It is like a Christian icon that exaggerates features in order to denote qualities too sublime for words. Ezekiel's description does the same thing; it reveals the sublime traits of these angels while at the same time hiding them under a shroud of mystery.

Zechariah 12:10-11 - Losing King Josiah: How the disciples mourned when Christ was pierced (May 29, 2015)

Hit movies love to use catchphrases. Some of these catchphrases become so memorable that one only has to repeat it and immediately the whole movie comes to mind. "I'll be back…" evokes the Terminator. "Play it again, Sam" evokes Casablanca.

In the first century, the Jews knew the Old Testament like we know hit movies. A single reference to an Old Testament text would immediately bring to mind the text referenced. In some rare cases, more than one text can be referenced. A fascinating example of this double-reference is found in the Gospel of John.

John recounts how, at the crucifixion, the Roman soldiers did not break Jesus' legs, but pierced his side with a lance. John says this was to fulfill two Old Testament passages: "Not a bone of it will be broken" (Exodus 12:46, Numbers 9:12) and "They will look upon him whom they have pierced" (Zechariah 12:10). The first text refers to the requirements for the Passover lamb. The second fulfillment refers to a prophecy in Zechariah. This second fulfillment is most interesting.

Zechariah 12:10-11 reads, "I will pour out on the house of David and on the inhabitants of Jerusalem, the Spirit of grace and of supplication, so that they will look on Me whom they have pierced; and they will mourn for Him, as one mourns for an only son, and they will weep bitterly over Him like the bitter weeping over a firstborn. In that day there will be great mourning in Jerusalem, like the mourning of Hadadrimmon in the plain of Megiddo."

What's interesting about this text is that the Hebrew and Latin speak in the first person — "They will look on *Me* whom they pierced" — who does "me" refer to? In context, it refers to God. God is pierced. For non-Christians, this causes a problem: How can God be pierced? For the Christian, this causes no problem because Christ is a Divine Person, the Second Person of the Trinity.

The last verse makes reference to yet another event: "... there will be great mourning in Jerusalem, like the mourning of Hadadrimmon in the plain of Megiddo." Everyone knows what happened in the plain of Megiddo, right? If you don't, trust me, you're not alone.

The plain of Megiddo is where one of the greatest kings of Judah, King Josiah, was fatally wounded. Josiah's reign was a time of great hope. Judah was a vassal of Assyria, which was growing weak. Josiah instituted a series of reforms that detached Judah from the clutches of Assyrian and native pagan worship. He destroyed the pagan idols and cleansed the temple of them (2 Kings 23:4-14) and reformed the priesthood (2 Kings 23:5). He also discovered "the book of the Law" in the Temple and re-inaugurated the covenant between God and His people (2 Kings 23:1-3, 2 Chronicles 24:29-33). He also revived the celebration of Passover (2 Kings 23:21-22, 2 Chronicles 35:1-35).

All these reforms stoked a nationalist feeling among the people with hopes that Judah would once again be freed from foreign domination. All this ended in 609 B.C., when Josiah ignored God's warning and set out to battle Neco II of Egypt in Megiddo. Josiah was fatally wounded and later died in Jerusalem. Judah's hopes were dashed.

Zechariah says such would be the mourning over the pierced one, and this connection could not be more accurate. Like Josiah, Jesus was a son of David. Where Josiah discovered the Law, Jesus disclosed the New Law at the Sermon on the Mount. Jesus cleansed the Temple and instituted the New Passover, where He made new priests, and He inaugurated a New Covenant.

Also just like Josiah, Christ's followers believed He would usher in an era of political independence. But they didn't understand that Christ came as the Suffering Servant, not the conquering King, and His death, being pierced by a sword, dashed all hopes of a political restoration just like in the days of Josiah.

This chain of references from John to Josiah really says a lot for only a few words.

Malachi 1:11 - "From the Rising of the Sun...": Every Mass is a Prophecy Fulfilled (May 12, 2016)

Here are two elements you probably never put together: The destruction of the Jerusalem Temple and Eucharistic Prayer No. 3. What does the third Eucharistic Prayer have to do with an event that took place in A.D. 70?

During the Mass, the priest, if he is using this prayer, will pray:

> "… you never cease to gather a people to yourself, so that from the rising of the sun to its setting a pure sacrifice may be offered to your name."

If you're Catholic, this passage sounds very familiar. But did you know this prayer quotes the Old Testament book of Malachi? The context of the passage is a bit sad. After God assures Israel of His love, He asks, "A son honors his father, and a servant fears his master; If then I am a father, where is the honor due to me? And if I am a master, where is the reverence due to me?" (Malachi 1:6).

How did Israel dishonor God? Instead of offering God the best of their flocks as sacrifices and signs of their love and fidelity to Him, they gave Him what they didn't want for themselves. They offered cattle that were blind, sick or lame. In a sense, they treated God's holy altar as a way to getting rid of their garbage. What's incredible is that even though they disrespected God in such a horrible way, they still expected Him to accept their sacrifices and answer their prayers. Malachi continues by giving this prophecy:

> "Oh, that one among you would shut the temple gates to keep you from kindling fire on my altar in vain! I have no pleasure in you, says the LORD of hosts; neither will I accept any sacrifice from your hands, For from the rising of the sun, even to its setting, my name is great among the nations; And everywhere they bring sacrifice to my name, and a pure offering; For great is my name among the nations, says the LORD of hosts."

Malachi predicted that instead of one place (Jerusalem) and one nation (the Jews) offering sacrifices to God, there would come a day when the nations around the world (i.e., "from the rising of the sun, even to its setting") would offer a pure and acceptable sacrifice.

In September of A.D. 70, the unthinkable happened. The Jerusalem temple was destroyed and the Jews would no longer offer the sacrifices prescribed in the Old Covenant. Jesus not only predicted the destruction of the temple by saying that there would not be left a "stone upon another stone" (Matthew 24:2; Mark

13:2, 16:3; Luke 19:44), but that the time was coming when people would no longer worship in Jerusalem (John 4:20). This because Jesus is greater than the temple (Matthew 12:6). Unlike the Jerusalem temple that would be torn down, the temple of Jesus' body would die and rise again (John 2:21) and the sacrifices offered in Jerusalem that could not take away sins (Hebrews 10:4) were fulfilled in Christ's sacrifice on the cross.

But Jesus' sacrifice happened only once on Calvary 2,000 years ago. Why, then, did Malachi prophesy that the nations everywhere would be offering a pure sacrifice? How was this second part of the prophecy fulfilled?

One of the earliest extra-biblical Christian writings we possess is called the *Didache* (or The Teaching). Notice what it says:

> "But every Lord's day, gather yourselves together and break bread, and give thanksgiving after having confessed your transgressions, that your sacrifice may be pure ... For this is that which was spoken by the Lord: In every place and time offer to me a pure sacrifice; for I am a great King, says the Lord, and my name is wonderful among the nations."

The imperfect and bloody sacrifices offered in the temple that couldn't take away sins were fulfilled in Christ's one perfect sacrifice to the Father on the Cross. That same sacrifice is represented on the altars around the world in the Eucharistic sacrifice of the Mass.

Therefore, every time the Holy Mass is offered, we are living out the fulfillment of Malachi's prophecy.

Song of Songs

The "Song of Songs" Journey to the Bible (Jan. 25, 2016)

Have you ever heard someone say, "I interpret the Bible literally"? When I hear this, I often wonder how they'd interpret the Song of Songs. After all, the Song of Songs is a love poem — and a pretty heated one at that.

What's unique about this book is that if one approaches it in a literalistic fashion, it doesn't really seem to be a religious book at all, much less a book one would expect to find in the Bible. But if it is interpreted allegorically, it becomes a very profound religious text.

The ancient rabbis understood the Song of Songs to be a love song between God and Israel. The early Church understood it as a passionate dialogue between Christ the Bridegroom and His bride, the Church. How one approaches the Song of Songs impacts the book's religious character, so the book had a bumpy journey into the Bible, at least within rabbinical Judaism.

Christians didn't have a problem with the sacredness of the Song of Songs. The earliest Christians were fond of interpreting the Old Testament allegorically, so the religious character of this book wasn't a matter of dispute. Moreover, the Song of Songs was included in the original deposit of faith given to the Church by Christ and his Apostles as a book that was to be read as sacred Scripture in the liturgy. With very rare exceptions, it was accepted by all and the Church solemnly affirmed it as canonical Scripture at the councils of Hippo (A.D. 393), Carthage (A.D. 419) Florence (A.D. 1442), and the Council of Trent (A.D. 1546). No problem here. However, the same can't be said for rabbinical Judaism.

Disputes concerning the sacredness of the Song of Songs continued into the second Christian century. In addition to disputes among the rabbis concerning the sacredness of this book, there appears to also have been abuse. One rabbinic text, for example, corrects those who use the Song of Songs in a profane manner: "He who recites a verse from the Song of Songs and treats it as a [secular] air, and one who recites a verse at a banquet table ... brings evil upon the world" (Sanhedrin 101a).

Eventually, a ruling needed to be made, and it appears to have come from Rabbi Akiba ben Joseph, the head of the rabbinical school in Jamnia sometime between A.D. 132-135. After listing the opinions of rabbis who disputed or affirm the sacredness of the Song of Songs and a few other books, Akiba exclaimed:

> "Heaven forbid. No man in Israel ever contended regarding the Song of Songs ... for the whole world is not worth the day when the Song of Songs was given to Israel ... for the Song of Songs is the most sacred of all of them [the Writings]" (Mishnah, Yahayim 3:5).

Akiba's hyperbolic statement that no man in Israel ever disputed the sacredness of the Song of Songs was intended to drive home a point: the Song of Songs is sacred, end of discussion!

Why did Akiba believe it was time to end the disputes? Before Akiba, Judaism didn't have a single *official* Old Testament text.

Different Jews used different texts. Many, for example, used a Greek translation of the Old Testament called the Septuagint. This is the preferred Old Testament text quoted in the New Testament.

But others used different texts and translations, much like Christians will use different English translations and texts today. However, there became a need to unify Judaism and adopt a single official Hebrew text that all Jews would use. This text would later be called the Masoretic Text. But there was a problem: The Masoretic Text would never become the norm if rabbis continued to dispute about certain books it contained. Therefore, Akiba put an end to any rabbinical doubts. As one rabbinical text puts it, "… [The] Song of Songs [was] 'hidden' until the men of the Great Assembly declared [it] to be written in the 'holy spirit'" (Avot R. Nathan 1:4).

Today, everybody (Catholic, Protestant, Orthodox, and Jews) accepts and enjoys the beauty of the passionate love God has for His people expressed in the Song of Songs.

THE DEUTEROCANON

Did the Jews Ever Accept the Deuterocanon? (November 10, 2016)

Time and again I run across anti-Catholic websites that claim (erroneously) that the Jews never accepted the Deuterocanon, or the seven Old Testament books that Catholics and Orthodox Christians accept as Scripture, but Protestants reject as "Apocrypha" (Tobit, Judith, Wisdom, Sirach/Ecclesiasticus, Baruch, 1 and 2 Maccabees, as well as parts of Esther and Daniel).

On the contrary, one could appeal to New Testament evidence that Jesus, the Apostles, and the inspired authors of the New Testament did indeed accept the Deuterocanon as Scripture. But does extra-biblical evidence exist that points to the earliest Christians' acceptance of these seven books?

One of the earliest pieces of evidence comes from a person who, despite his hostility toward Christianity, nevertheless attests to a few truths of the budding faith, including the acceptance of the Deuterocanon.

After the First Jewish Revolt (AD 66-73), the rabbinical school in Jamnia became *the* center for Jewish religious and political thought. The destruction of the Jerusalem Temple during the First Revolt left Judaism in a precarious position, since it was impossible for the Jews to follow all the cultic requirements of the Old Testament ceremonial law without the presence of the Temple. Two paths laid before the nation: either stage a second revolt and rebuild the

Temple, or redefine Judaism from a cultic religion to a religion of the book. Rabbi Akiba be Joseph (A.D. 37-137), the head of the school during the first decades of the second Christian century, endorsed both paths.

Rabbi Akiba is perhaps best known in history as the rabbi who endorsed a false messiah. According to Akiba, the messiah promised in Numbers 24:7 who would defeat the Romans, rebuild the Temple and rule as the messianic king was personified in a man named Simon bar Kokhba. Akiba's endorsement of bar Kokhba changed the complexion of the Second Jewish Revolt (AD 132-135), turning it from a popular uprising into a messianic movement.

Large numbers of Jews and even pagans joined the revolt, but a small segment known as the Christians refused to take part, since it would be tantamount to rejecting Jesus as the true messiah. As a result, the Jews saw Christianity not only as a heresy, but as sedition, too. Needless to say, Akiba was a false prophet. Bar Kokhba wasn't the messiah, and the consequences of the failed Second Revolt were horrific: Simon bar Kokhba was killed, Rabbi Akiba was martyred, and the reprisals by the Romans almost wiped Judaism off the map.

The second path Akiba endorsed included the redefinition of Judaism along non-sacrificial lines, at least until the Temple was restored. To do so, Akiba used a creative style of biblical interpretation to read into the Hebrew text whatever he needed. The only problem was that the Jews never *had* a single normative biblical text. Therefore, the first order of business was to adopt single text for the Rabbinical Bible. It is here that Rabbi Akiba inadvertently reveals something about Deuterocanon.

In a work called Tosefta Yadayim, 2:13, Akiba says: "The Gospels and heretical books do not defile the hands. The books of Ben Sira and all other books written from then on, do not defile the hands."

The phrase "do not defile the hands" refers to a non-sacred text. Therefore, Akiba is stating that the Christian Scriptures are not sacred — no surprise there — and the "books of ben Sira and all other books written from then on" are not sacred. The book of Sirach is the oldest book of the Deuterocanon. Therefore, Akiba's decree rejects the whole of the Deuterocanon as inspired Scripture.

Inadvertently, though, what Akiba's statement *does* show is that a sizeable number of Jewish Christians *did* accept the Deuterocanon as Scripture in Akiba's day (i.e., before AD 132), in order for the noted rabbi to associate it with the Christian Scriptures. He must also have believed there was the potential for non-Christian Jews to have accepted it as sacred Scripture; otherwise, there would be no need for his ruling. Despite his opposition to the Catholic faith, Rabbi Akiba unintentionally becomes a hostile witness that the early Jewish Christians believed that the Deuterocanon was, in fact, Scripture.

Who Wrote the Books of Solomon? (October 30, 2014)

Remember the old television show "You Bet Your Life?" Groucho used to ask the losing contestant a question that was impossible to get wrong, like "Who's buried in Grant's tomb?" Grant is buried in Grant's tomb, obviously. But what if someone asked you, "Who wrote the books of Solomon?" Would you answer Solomon? If you did, you'd be wrong, at least partially.

Solomon, as you may know, is one of the most noteworthy people in the Old Testament. He was the son of King David and reigned over Israel for 40 years (1 Kings 11:42). He built the Jerusalem Temple and expanded Israel's power and influence far and wide. But he is most known for his wisdom. Instead of asking God for a long life or riches, Solomon asked God for wisdom, and God granted his prayer in abundance (1 Kings 3:4-15). By the end of his life, Solomon produced 3,000 proverbs and 1,005 songs (2 Kings 5:12). That's a lot of wisdom!

Solomon's renown for wisdom also left a mark on how we look at the Bible. The Bible isn't a single book, but a collection of books in one volume. And like libraries today are categorized into topics, so too with the books of the Bible. For example, we have the "books of Moses" (Genesis, Exodus, Leviticus, Numbers and Deuteronomy), the four "books of Kings" or "Kingdoms" (1st and 2nd Samuel, 1st and 2nd Kings), the major prophets, the minor prophets, and the five books of Solomon (Proverbs, Ecclesiastes, Song of Songs, Wisdom of Solomon, and Sirach).

At first glance, this last grouping may seem odd. After all, the son of Sirach wrote Sirach, not Solomon. Why would Sirach be counted among the books of Solomon? Didn't the early Church Fathers notice this problem? They certainly did. They knew Solomon didn't write Sirach just as they knew that the book of Wisdom was not a direct composition of Solomon (some believed Philo of Alexandria, a Jewish philosopher, put the book together). But if you want to get technical, even the books that were written by Solomon weren't totally Solomon's work. For example, Proverbs includes the words of Agur (Proverb 30:1-6) and Lemuel (Proverbs 31:1-9). So if Solomon didn't write all of the "books of Solomon," why did the early Fathers group these books under that title?

For the ancients, Solomon's notoriety for wisdom made him, in some sense, the obvious patron of these books; all of them were influenced by him, if not in their contents, in their eloquence and style. Read sections of Proverbs, Wisdom, and Sirach one after the other and you'll see what I mean. Therefore, these five books became known as those "of Solomon."

This type of grouping under a person's name shouldn't be too surprising. We see a similar thing happening with the book of Psalms. The Psalms are often called "the Psalms of David." And indeed, David did write a majority of the Psalms, but, like Solomon's Proverbs, other people contributed as well, such as Moses (Psalm 89), Solomon (Psalms 71 and 126), the sons of Core (Psalm 41-48, 83, 84, 86), Eman (Psalm 87), Ethan (Psalm 88), Asaph (Psalm 49, 72-82), and so on. David became known for his Psalm and therefore the books of Psalms were called "the Psalms of David." Jeremiah, likewise, had a group of books, namely, the book of Jeremiah, Baruch, and the Letter of Jeremiah. The early Church often referred to these three works as those "of Jeremiah" even though they knew that Baruch wrote Baruch.

So, who then wrote the "books of Solomon?" Tradition affirms that Solomon is the substantial human author of Proverbs, Ecclesiastes, and the Song of Songs. Sirach and Wisdom are "of Solomon" largely because they share the same eloquence and style as those of Solomon. So, the next time you want to try to stump your Bible study teacher, ask "Who wrote the books of Solomon?" and see what they say.

Wisdom 7:27 - The Wisdom behind "God from God, Light from Light" (June 27, 2014)

Although every Church council is important, the council of Nicaea holds a privileged place since it produced one of the most important summaries (or symbols) of our faith, the Nicene Creed. Catholics are familiar with this creed, as it is recited at Mass.

The contents are easy to understand. "We believe in one God, the Father almighty... (And) in one Lord, Jesus Christ, the Son of God..." But one line describes the Son as, "God from God, Light from Light, true God from true God." What does "light from light" mean? And why did the council fathers use this illustration?

What many Christians don't realize is that this description is drawn from the Old Testament deuterocanonical book of Wisdom. When we refer to a "deuterocanonical" book, we're referring to one of seven Old Testament books —Wisdom, Sirach, Baruch, Tobit, Judith, 1st and 2nd Maccabees (as well as sections of Esther and Daniel) — that weren't included in the Jewish text about 60 years after the destruction of the Jerusalem Temple in 70 A.D. These books, however, have always been included in Catholic and Orthodox Bibles, although most Protestant Bibles today do not include them.

The closest New Testament reference to "light from light" is found in the Epistle to the Hebrews. The Epistle begins by stating how God spoke in partial and various ways through the prophets, but now He has spoken definitively through His Son (Hebrews 1:1-2). Verse 3 describes the pre-incarnate Son's relationship to the Father:

> "[the Son]… is the refulgence of his [the Father's] glory, the very imprint of his being."

"Refulgence," or "brightness" (Greek, apaugasma), is a very rare Greek word in the Bible. In fact, the Greek Bible only uses it twice, here in Hebrews 1:3 and in Wisdom 7:26. This is no accident. The chapter in Wisdom is a lengthy description of God's Wisdom and its relationship to God and creation. Wisdom (the Son) is the artificer of all (cf. Hebrews 1:2 and Wisdom 7:22). Wisdom (the Son) holds all things in being (cf. Hebrews 1:3 and Wisdom 4:1). But most importantly, Wisdom's relationship to God is likened to the splendor of light: *"the refulgence of [God's] eternal light, the spotless mirror of the power of God, the image of his goodness" (Wisdom 7:26)*.

Since the Eternal Son is elsewhere identified as God's wisdom and power (1 Corinthians 3:24), it shouldn't surprise anyone to see the author of Hebrews using this illustration from Wisdom to describe the Son's relationship to the Father.

But what does this tell us about the Father and the Son? Quite a bit. The early Church fathers understood these texts to teach that both the Father and the Son existed eternally; they are co-eternal. Why? Could a flame exist without its refulgence or brightness? No, of course not. The flame and its brightness co-exist. Wisdom 7:26 likens God to an eternal light, a light with no beginning and no end. If God's Wisdom is the eternal light's brightness, than God's Wisdom is eternal as well.

The Father was never without the Son, nor was the Son without the Father. The early fathers repeatedly used this text against a heresy that denied that the Son was co-eternal with the Father. St. Augustine mocked such an idea. After quoting Wisdom 7:26,

Augustine wrote, "Are you seeking for a Son without a Father? Give me a light without brightness..." (*Sermons on Selected N.T. Lessons*, 68, 2).

The precision of this analogy is remarkable. It's no wonder it found its way into the Nicene creed. So the next time you recite the creed knowing the biblical background of "light from light," just think of Wisdom.

Wisdom 8:1 - The Wisdom of Science (December 8, 2016)

"O come, thou Wisdom from on high, who orders all things mightily..." This line is from the second verse of "O Come, O Come Emmanuel." What most people don't know is that it is a quote from the deuterocanonical book of Wisdom, which reads, "Indeed, she [God's Wisdom] reaches from end to end mightily and governs all things well" (Wisdom 8:1). What even fewer people know is that this verse and a few other passages from the Old Testament Deuterocanon supplied several necessary components for the birth of modern science.

Before science could get off the ground as a self-sustaining enterprise, it needed to be grounded in a correct understanding of reality. This grounding occurred between 250 B.C. and 50 B.C., when the Greeks were forcing the Jews to accept various elements of Greek culture. This clash of civilizations resulted in both an armed uprising (chronicled in 1st and 2nd Maccabees) and theological exposition (especially in the Book of Wisdom). It is against this Hellenizing backdrop that these inspired authors reasserted Jewish theology in light of the onslaught of Greek ideas.

The result was a correct understanding of reality that later became the fertile soil in which science could grow.

One important correction was made in the area of understanding time. The Greeks, and many other ancient cultures, believed time was an eternally repeating cycle. What we do today will be done again eons from now, and so on. The mother of the Maccabean martyrs corrects this mistaken notion when she said, "I beg you, child, to look at the heavens and the earth and see all that is in them; then you will know that God did not make them out of existing things..." (2 Maccabees 7:28). If God created everything from nothing, then it has a beginning that cannot be repeated.

The Book of Wisdom supplies a second and more important idea. Centuries earlier, Greek philosophers had noticed a rather strange correlation between notions that can be "seen" with our minds that do not exist in nature (i.e., numbers, proportions, etc.) and nature itself. These notions (or abstractions) had an uncanny application to things around us. So uncanny, in fact, that the Greek philosopher Pythagoras and others believed that numbers were the most basic or fundamental element of all things. Nature can be known and understood (at least to some degree) through reason.

The book of Wisdom confirms this relationship and goes one step further when it says, "...But you [God] have disposed all things by measure and number and weight" (Wisdom 11:20). The reason why these abstracts can be applied to nature is because the Creator has disposed all things to reflect His wisdom. God's Wisdom orders and governs all things mightily (Wisdom 8:1).

But if the Greeks were the first to make this connection, how can the Deuterocanon be said to have provided the foundation for science as a self-sustaining enterprise? The reason is because the Book of Wisdom supplied two things that philosophy could not: First, the philosophy of Pythagoras was just that, a philosophy. People were free to accept it or reject it for some other human philosophy, and many did. The Book of Wisdom is different. It is the inspired word of God. Therefore, whatever it says must be so. Nature doesn't just seem to be able to be understood by numbers and proportions; it must be able to be understood because God has made it so. The Deuterocanon, in other words, supplies an imperative that human philosophy or speculation could not. Second, the Deuterocanon supplies the motivation to do science in the first place. The wise God created and disposed all things to reflect His wisdom. Since Christ is the "Power and Wisdom of God" (1 Corinthians 1:24) who orders all things mightily (Wisdom 8:1), investigating nature is just another way of seeing and adoring God's Wisdom as exhibited and reflected in nature.

It was no accident that Wisdom 11:20 was the most quoted Scripture by natural scientists throughout the Middle Ages. It was their marching orders. Remember this the next time you sing "O Come, O Come Emmanuel."

THE NEW TESTAMENT

The Four Gospels: What Sets Them Apart from the Rest?

From time to time we will hear about other "gospels" that circulated in the early Church. They are sometimes called "the Lost Gospels," but the fact of the matter is that these writings never were lost; they just never were accepted.

Dozens of so-called "gospels" circulated in the early Church, many of them with authoritative-sounding titles such as the "Gospel of Peter," the "Acts of Paul," and even a "Gospel of Judas." These so-called "gospels" are nothing new. They've been known for centuries as "apocryphal gospels" — works of fiction that were not considered Scripture.

At best, some of the early apocryphal works are pious stories that may contain a grain of truth, such as the Protoevangelium of James. At worst, others were attempts to wrap a sect's strange, esoteric, and heretical doctrine inside the cloak of apostolic approval.

Able to tell the difference, the early Church wasn't fooled, for the simple reason that the apocryphal gospels lack the necessary pedigree to be considered Scripture. Most, with rare exceptions, came too late — sometimes centuries after apostolic times — to ever be considered authentic. Moreover, they never were universally accepted throughout the Church; many of them circulated only in a particular region or among the members of a particular sect.

The four authentic Gospels were different. All of them were written well within the first century. Since none of them mention the fulfillment of Christ's prophecy about the destruction of the temple (which occurred in A.D. 70), scholars have suggested that all four Gospels may have been written prior to that event.

Moreover, the earliest Christians, whose lives and well-being were tied to the truthfulness of the Gospel, received only four Gospels (Matthew, Mark, Luke and John), no more and no less. Several early Christian writers recognized this: For example, St. Irenaeus of Lyon (who was a disciple of St. Polycarp, who was a disciple of John the Apostle) wrote this around A.D. 180:

> "There are four gospels and only four, neither more nor less: four like the points of the compass, four like the chief directions of the wind. The Church, spread all over the world, has in the gospels four pillars and four winds blowing wherever people live" (Against Heresies, 3, 11, 8).

Roughly a decade earlier, a Christian writer named Tatian composed a work called the Diatessaron. In it, Tatian attempted to harmonize the Gospels into a single narrative — using only the four Gospels we recognize as authentic today.

Twenty years earlier, around A.D. 150, St. Justin attests to the apostolic roots of the Gospels when he mentions them as the "memoirs" of the Apostles:

> "For the apostles, in the memoirs composed by them, which are called Gospels, have thus delivered unto us what was enjoined upon them; that Jesus took bread, and when He had given

thanks, said, 'This do ye in remembrance of Me...'" (First Apology, 66).

Although Justin does not mention how many Gospels there were, we do know that Tatian (mentioned above) was St. Justin's disciple and his Diatessaron harmonized four (and only four) Gospels, so we can safely assume Justin believed the same.

You might be familiar with the idea of the four Gospel-writing evangelists being symbolized by the face of a lion, an ox, a man and an eagle — this very fact is a testament to there being four Gospels, and only four. St. Irenaeus noted that the four Gospels put forward four different aspects of Christ that match the faces of cherubs in Ezekiel 1:10. According to Irenaeus, John's Gospel begins with Christ's kingly Sonship as "the Word" (giving him the kingly symbol of a lion). Luke begins with Zechariah's offering sacrifice (giving him the sacrificial symbol of an ox). Matthew begins with Christ's human genealogy (giving him the face of a man), and Mark begins with the calling on the prophetic Spirit from on high (represented by the eagle).

Which Old Testament Did Jesus Use, Anyway? (December 12, 2014)

During a radio interview, someone called in and asked me for a recommendation on a good English translation of the Hebrew Old Testament. The caller said she wanted to go back to the ancient roots of her faith and thought reading the Hebrew text was the way to go. My answer probably surprised her.

I told her that if she wanted to get back to the "old-time religion," she should use the Scripture that Jesus, St. Paul, and the writers of the New Testament most commonly used, but it wasn't Hebrew. It was Greek.

Greek? Wasn't the Old Testament for the most part originally written in Hebrew? Didn't the New Testament rely on the Hebrew Old Testament? To answer this, we need to take a closer look at what's going on behind the Bible.

There were a number of different Old Testament texts in circulation in the first century. Some were written in Hebrew, while others were translations of the Hebrew into Aramaic and Greek. The one text that the writers of the New Testament appear to have favored more than the others is a Greek translation known as the Septuagint.

The Septuagint got its rather odd name from a story found in the Letter of Aristeas that relates how 70 (perhaps 72) Jewish scribes were commissioned to translate the Old Testament into Greek during the reign of Ptolemy II Philadelphus (309–246 B.C.). According to the story, these 70 scribes worked separately on their translations, yet they miraculously translated the exact same thing, word for word. Hence, it is called the Seventy, which in Latin is Septuagint (or LXX for short).

Although the New Testament used texts other than the Septuagint, it certainly quotes from it more than the others. In fact, the Septuagint makes up about two-thirds of the approximately 300 Old Testament quotations made in the New Testament. Some of these quotations are quite important.

Perhaps the most famous New Testament quotations from the Septuagint is found in Matthew 1:22-23, where it says of Christ's birth, "All this took place to fulfill what the Lord had said through the prophet: 'Behold, the virgin shall be with child and bear a son, and they shall name him Emmanuel,' which means 'God is with us'" (Isaiah 7:14 LXX).

What's significant about this quotation is that the Hebrew text that has come down to us gives a rather general word, usually translated "young maiden," instead of the Septuagint's "virgin." Of course, young maidens can be virgins (as normally would be the case), but the word doesn't have that specific of a meaning. This difference, I believe, highlights the real value of the Greek Septuagint for understanding the New Testament and first century Judaism.

What's amazing about the Septuagint is that it can function as a snapshot of how the Jews understood the Hebrew text hundreds of years before the time of Christ. Remember, the Septuagint was translated some time before the late second century B.C. When the translators came across Isaiah 7:14, which Matthew quoted above, they translated the word as "virgin" showing that in their day the "young maiden" of Isaiah 7:14 was understood to be a virgin. Matthew, therefore, understood that Mary's virgin birth of Jesus was the fulfillment of Isaiah 7:14, as it was understood in pre-Christian Judaism.

Much later, around the middle of the second Christian century, when rabbinical Judaism adopted a Hebrew text to be their norm, they rejected the Septuagint. But Christians continued to use what they've always used, the Greek Septuagint.

So if you'd like to get back to that "old time religion," you'd do what Jesus, the Apostles, the New Testament writers and the early Church did; you'd go to the Septuagint.

The Gospel According to Matthew

Matthew 2:16 - Did Herod Slaughter the Holy Innocents? (December 21, 2016)

At the beginning of Matthew's Gospel, we read how King Herod learned from the Magi that the messiah king had been born. Herod told the Magi to return and let him know where they found the infant so that he could also pay him homage. The Magi saw through Herod's deception and returned by a different route. Enraged, Herod ordered that every male child two years old and under in Bethlehem and its vicinity be killed (Matthew 2:16). The Church commemorates this event with the Feast of the Holy Innocents on Dec. 28 in the west and Dec. 29 in the east.

But did this tragedy actually occur? There are some who hold that the death of the Holy Innocents is little more than a pious fiction, but is that the case?

When we look at the background of this text, we find that the events recorded ring true. Herod was installed as king of Judah, not by the Jewish populace, but by the pagan Romans. In fact, Herod was an Edomite, which meant that in the eyes of the Jews he had no right to be their king because God promised David that his descendants would sit on the throne forever.

Therefore, Herod would not have been overjoyed to hear of the recent birth of the messiah king in Bethlehem. Quite the opposite. Herod would have seen Christ's birth as a threat to his throne. Herod's murderous response also fits our knowledge of Herod. He murdered several of his own family members because he suspected disloyalty — causing Caesar Augustus to quip that "It is better to be Herod's pig than a son." Murdering these young children is perfectly in keeping with everything we know about Herod. Why, then, do some doubt?

The arguments against the historicity of this event are based almost entirely on silence, particularly the silence of a first century Jewish historian named Josephus. Josephus provides us with several details about Herod's life and works, but never mentions the murder of the Holy Innocents. It is assumed, therefore, that the event must never have happened. But is this conclusion sound?

Part of the problem is it was once thought that the number of children murdered ran into the thousands and therefore the scale of the tragedy couldn't have escaped Josephus' attention, if it did happen. But more recent research has shown that the actual number would have been considerably smaller, perhaps less than 20 children killed. The figure is still large, but compared to the carnage Herod wrought during his reign, Josephus could have omitted it without any trouble.

Moreover, it is clear from Josephus' other treatments of historic figures that he never intended to given an exhaustive account of his subjects. For example, Josephus's description of the Essenes, the Jewish group famous for producing the Dead Sea Scrolls, entirely omits any mention of the group's apocalyptic worldview, which was its hallmark. Therefore, if the first century Jewish historian chose not to give an exhaustive account of the acts of Herod, there is no reason to suspect the historicity of anything omitted by him.

There is also another plausible reason for Josephus's omission of this event; he may not have connected Herod with the murders in Bethlehem. There's nothing in Matthew that suggests that Herod sent his own troops to kill these children. In fact, Matthew 2:16 only says that Herod "...sent and killed" the children. It's quite possible that Herod did not send his own troops (making it an official act), but rather sent banditti to do his bidding. A very ancient extra-biblical text known as the Protoevangelium of James seems to support this idea. In chapter 22, the text says, "And when Herod knew that he had been mocked by the Magi, in a rage he sent murderers, saying to them: Slay the children from two years old and under."

For Christians who knew what transpired with the Magi, Herod's role in the Bethlehem tragedy would have been obvious, but for a later Jewish historian who wouldn't have known this information the tragedy in Bethlehem would have been seemed like just another senseless act of brutality common for the era.

Matthew 1:23 - Who was to Conceive: A Virgin or a Simply a 'Young Maiden"? (Dec. 22, 2015)

Few passages in Scripture have been as hotly contested by non-Christians as Matthew 1:23, "Behold, the virgin shall be with child and bear a son, and they shall name him Emmanuel ..." Jewish writers and even the so-called "new atheists" accuse St. Matthew of not knowing Hebrew and thereby mistranslating Isaiah 7:14's Hebrew word *almah* as "the *virgin* shall conceive ..." instead of "*young maiden.*"

What these critics fail to notice is that Matthew isn't translating Isaiah 7:14; he's copying it from an ancient Greek translation of the Old Testament called the Septuagint. The Septuagint translated *almah* as "virgin," not Matthew. Moreover, the Septuagint was a Jewish translation, so it would be a very odd charge indeed to accuse these ancient Jews of not knowing Hebrew.

But why does the Hebrew say "young maiden" instead of "virgin?" The answer appears to be that there was no Hebrew word that directly and exclusively referenced virgins. Therefore, another word would be needed to make the point indirectly. Because it was the cultural norm that young unmarried girls were virgins, *almah* was a good substitute.

If this is so, how did the Septuagint know that *almah* in Isaiah 7:14 specifically meant "virgin," and not the more general "young maiden?" That's a question only answered by the translators. However, if one looks at what was going on during the time when Isaiah was translated, we might find a clue.

Work on the Septuagint began roughly around 200 B.C. starting with the Torah (the first five books of the Bible) and the rest of the books were translated afterward until around the time of Christ. Something remarkable happened during this period that few people outside of scholarly circles know.

God had promised David that his dynasty and kingdom would last forever (1 Samuel 7:16), but through the disobedience of Solomon and subsequent kings, David's kingdom of twelve tribes became divided into two kingdoms, and both were eventually sent into exile. The 10 northern tribes of Israel never fully returned, and the two tribes of Judah came back, but without a king and under the oppression of foreign powers.

After Alexander the Great (332 B.C.), the Seleucids controlled Judea until the Jews eventually rose up and pushed back against the Greeks. What happened next from the perspective of a pious Jew at the time was nothing short of a miracle. The Seleucid empire began to collapse, and the Jews once again slowly took charge of their own land. By the time the dust settled, almost the entire former territory of David's kingdom was under Jewish control. God was restoring Israel! But there was one problem: the kings who ruled during this period weren't Davidic; they were Hasmonean. The promise of restoration was given to David's son, not to a Hasmonean. How was God going to restart David's dynasty when there was no king to bestow the promise that his son would sit on the throne?

The translators of the Septuagint might have had this question in mind when they translated Isaiah 7, which addresses a dynastic crisis back in Isaiah's day. The northern kingdom of Israel and Damascus were threatening to invade Judah and replace David's descendent, King Ahaz, with a non-Davidic puppet king, a certain "son of Tabeel" (Isaiah 7:6). Isaiah tells Ahaz that God will not allow it, and as a sign that the fall of David's dynasty would not take place, "the *almah* will conceive and bear a son …"

It's possible that when the Jewish translators looked at Isaiah 7:14, they saw the key to understanding how God would bring back David's dynastic heir. The remarkable sign wasn't that a young maiden would have a son — that's not very momentous — but that a *virgin* would have a son.

Because God is the true king of Israel (1 Samuel 8:7), he could, one day, promise a virgin that her child would take "the throne of David his father" (Luke 1:32-33). The questions raised by Hasmonean kings might have provided the Greek translators of Isaiah a crucial insight into what made Isaiah's "young maiden" so remarkable: she must be a virgin.

Matthew 1:25 - Small Words Can Cause Big Problems (March 31, 2015)

It's funny how some of the smallest things can cause the biggest problems. Take, for example, the little word "until." It's a very common word. You've probably read thousands of sentences that use "until" and never gave it much thought. But in the realm of theology and Scripture study, little words can sometimes cause big problems if they're misunderstood. Such is the case in Matthew's Gospel, where this little unpretentious word has caused many to misunderstand the Blessed Virgin Mary.

After being visited in a dream informing him that Jesus was conceived by the power of the Holy Spirit, Matthew 1:25 states that Joseph "... had no relations with her until she bore a son." Protestants often argue that because the word "until" implies a change occurs after Jesus' birth, Joseph must have had normal marital relations with his wife afterward, denying Mary's perpetual virginity. Is this biblical or is there more to the word "until" than meets the eye?

While the word "until" often indicates a change after a certain period of time, it doesn't have to. For example, when we say, "He was put in police custody until he stood trial," obviously we don't mean that the prisoner was released once the trial began. He remained in custody during the trial and possibly afterward as well.

Parallel examples can be found in Scripture, as well. In Acts 25:21, Festus tells King Agrippa that Paul was put in custody until he could be sent to Caesar. Obviously, this doesn't imply that once Paul was sent to Caesar he was released from custody. The Apostle remained in protective custody even after he arrived in Rome. The "until" in Acts 25:21, therefore, does not signal that a change took place, but rather only comments on the state of affairs up until Festus sent Paul to Caesar.

There are many other biblical examples of this focused use of "until." One of my favorites is in 2 Samuel, which says, "And Michal the daughter of Saul had no child till the day of her death" (2 Samuel 6:23). Obviously, Michal didn't give birth to a child after she died! The "until" merely states that Michal remained childless for the rest of her life.

Another favorite is 1 Timothy 4:13, where Paul commands Timothy, "Until I come, attend to the public reading of Scripture, to preaching, to teaching." If "until" always signals a change, then Paul must have meant Timothy to stop publicly reading Scripture, preaching, and teaching after he arrived, which is nonsense. Paul's concern is that Timothy should continue to do these things before he comes. He was not implying anything about what would happen after he arrived. The same is true for the "until" in Matthew 1:25.

Matthew's concern is to establish the Virgin Birth. Matthew 1:18 introduces this section with, "...[This is] how the birth of Jesus Christ came about. When his mother Mary was betrothed to Joseph, but before they lived together, she was found with child through the holy Spirit..." He then recounts how the angel informed Joseph of this in a dream (Matthew 1:20-21) and how Christ's miraculous conception fulfills Isaiah 7:14, which says, "...a virgin shall conceive and bear a son..." (Matthew 1:23). Since the preceding context focuses exclusively on "how the birth of Jesus Christ came about," we have every reason to understand that the "until" in Matthew 1:25 speaks only to what happens before Jesus' birth, not afterward. Matthew 1:25, therefore, is evidence for the Virgin Birth, not a defeater for Mary's virginity.

Matthew 4:1-11 - Why Did Jesus Fast for 40 Days in the Desert? (February 18, 2016)

Did you ever wonder why the solemn season of Lent is 40 days long? I think most Catholics know the answer: "By the solemn forty days of Lent the Church unites herself each year to the mystery of Jesus in the desert" (CCC 540). Jesus fasted for 40 days and nights and so do we, but this still leaves the question: why 40?

If we look at Jesus' temptation in the desert in Matthew 4:1-11, we find a few clues. Each time Jesus responds to the devil, he replies with Scripture. When the devil says, "Turn these stones to bread," Jesus quotes Deuteronomy 8:3: "One does not live by bread alone, but by every word that comes forth from the mouth of God." When the devil tell Jesus to throw himself down from the temple, Jesus replies with Deuteronomy 6:16: "You shall not put the Lord your God to the test." When the devil commands Jesus to worships him, Jesus replies with Deuteronomy 6:13 (10:20): "The Lord, your God, shall you worship and him alone shall you serve."

Deuteronomy! Deuteronomy! Deuteronomy! Could the answer to "why 40 days?" be found in Deuteronomy?

The number 40 does come up in Deuteronomy in some pretty significant ways. For example, Moses twice fasts for 40 days. The first time is when he was preparing himself to receive the Ten Commandments to give to Israel at the base of the mountain (Deuteronomy 9:9-11). Curiously, Jesus gives the New Law on the Sermon on the Mount shortly after his 40-day fast (Matthew 5).

The second time Moses fasts for 40 days comes immediately after he gives the law. Moses returned from the mountain to find the Israelites worshipping the golden calf. God wished to wipe out Israel and make Moses into an even mightier nation (Deuteronomy 9:14), but Moses — being a good mediator — fasted another 40 days for the sins of his people (Deuteronomy 9:18).

Afterward, God permitted Israel to continue to the promised land (Deuteronomy 10:10-11).

Once there, the people rebelled again. They doubted whether they could overcome the inhabitants, so they sent scouts to assess their chances. After 40 days the scouts returned, saying it was impossible. Their discouraging report caused to people to rise up in rebellion.

Their punishment for this rebellion? Forty years in the desert. One year for each day their scouts reconnoitered the land (Number 14:34). Wandering 40 years in the desert was a period of testing, to "find out whether or not it was your intention to keep his commandments" (Deuteronomy 8:2). But during this trial, the

Israelites had to rely wholly on the Lord: "…Your clothes did not fall from you in tatters nor your sandals from your feet; bread was not your food, nor wine or beer your drink. Thus you should know that I, the LORD, am your God.'" (Deuteronomy 29:4-5).

Deuteronomy shows us that Jesus is a new Moses who after fasting for 40 days gives us a New Law and suffers for the sins of the people. He is also like a new Israel. Unlike the Israelites who fell repeatedly in the desert, Jesus response to temptation with the same words with which they should have responded.

By uniting ourselves with the mystery of Christ's trial in the desert, we're reminded that the 40 days of Lent are like our journey through the desert in this life. If we remain faithful, following the new Moses, Jesus Christ, we too will enter into the true promised land of heaven.

Matthew 8:24-28 - Master of the Seas: Who Calms the Waters? (November 13, 2015)

Did Jesus claim to be God? This is an important question, not only for our own personal faith, but also for defending that faith. Most people are familiar with New Testament texts that assert Christ's divinity (John 1:1, etc.), but there is much more evidence than people suppose — for example, when Christ calms the sea.

> Matthew 8:24-28: "Suddenly a violent storm came up on the sea, so that the boat was being swamped by waves; but he was asleep. They came and woke him, saying, 'Lord, save us! We are perishing!' He

> said to them, 'Why are you terrified, O you of little faith?' Then he got up, rebuked the winds and the sea, and there was great calm. The men were amazed and said, 'What sort of man is this, whom even the winds and the sea obey?'"

On the surface, Jesus is clearly exercising power that is beyond human nature. But what is this power? Someone could assert that angels are powerful, so maybe Jesus is exercising preternatural angelic power. What is it about this miracle that points to Christ's divinity?

The answer lies in the Old Testament background: who calms the waters? The Old Testament is quite clear on this point. Job 26:11-12, for example, says "The pillars of the heavens tremble and are stunned at his [God's] thunderous rebuke; By his power he stirs up the sea, and by his might he crushes Rahab ..." God stirs the sea to crush Rahab.

> Psalm 89:9-10 places the power to "rule the raging sea" and "still its swelling waves" exclusively in God's hands: "LORD, God of hosts, who is like you? Mighty LORD, your loyalty is always present. You rule the raging sea; you still its swelling waves."

Psalm 93:2 states that God's power exceeds that of the raging sea: "The flood has raised up, LORD; the flood has raised up its roar; the flood has raised its pounding waves. More powerful than the roar of many waters, more powerful than the breakers of the sea, powerful in the heavens is the LORD."

Even more remarkable is Psalm 107:23-31's description of sailors caught in a tempest:

> "Some went off to sea in ships, plied their trade on the deep waters. They saw the works of the LORD, the wonders of God in the deep. He spoke and roused a storm wind; it tossed the waves on high. They rose up to the heavens, sank to the depths; their hearts trembled at the danger. They reeled, staggered like drunkards; their skill was of no avail. In their distress they cried to the LORD, who brought them out of their peril, hushed the storm to a murmur; the waves of the sea were stilled. They rejoiced that the sea grew calm, that God brought them to the harbor they longed for."

As you probably noticed, there are several parallels between this Psalm and Matthew. Both passages speak of those caught in a fierce storm at sea. Both Christ's disciples and the sailors in the Psalm cry to the Lord. The sailors in Psalm 107:28 cried out to Yahweh where the disciples in Matthew 8:25 came to Jesus exclaiming, "Lord, save us! We are perishing!" The sea is calmed in both passages. In Psalm 107:28-29, God brings the sailors out of peril, and in Matthew 8:26 Jesus rescues them by rebuking the wind and the sea.

What's interesting is that the sailors in Psalm 107:31 knew who rescued them. They rejoiced "... that God brought them to the harbor they longed for." But not so with the disciples. They knew Job and the Psalms, so they knew that God rules the winds and the sea, but they had just witnessed Jesus doing what God does. They asked, "What sort of man is this, whom even the winds and the sea obey?"

That question brought them face to face with the mystery of the Incarnation. They knew Jesus to be man, but God rules the sea. How can Jesus calm the sea? This miracle is one of several steps along the way that led the disciples to eventually embrace Christ as true God and true man.

Matthew 12:32 - Why is Speaking Against the Holy Spirit an Unforgivable Sin? (Dec. 10, 2015)

In this age of Divine Mercy, we celebrate that "… God proves his love for us in that while we were still sinners Christ died for us" (Romans 5:8) and "If we acknowledge our sins, he is faithful and just and will forgive our sins and cleanse us from every wrongdoing" (1 John 1:9). Nothing is outside of God's mercy because God is love (1 John 4:8). No sin, no matter how great, is unforgivable.

But doesn't Jesus say that speaking against the Holy Spirit is an unforgivable sin?

"And whoever speaks a word against the Son of Man will be forgiven; but whoever speaks against the holy Spirit will not be forgiven, either in this age or in the age to come" (Matthew 12:32).

Why is speaking against the Son of Man (the Second Person of the Trinity) potentially forgivable, but doing the same against the Holy Spirit (the Third Person of the Trinity) unforgivable? Also, if God's mercy is greater than our sins, why is this sin unforgivable? Why is God unwilling to forgive it?

The preceding context provides some answers. In Matthew 12, Jesus has three rather heated encounters with the Pharisees. The first encounter concerns picking grain on the Sabbath (Matthew 12:1). The Pharisees objected, saying, "See, your disciples are doing what is unlawful to do on the Sabbath" (Matthew 12:2). Jesus replies that the priests work on the Sabbath without violating the Law (Matthew 12:3-8) and closes by quoting Hosea 6:6, "I desire mercy, not sacrifice."

The second encounter concerns healing on the Sabbath (Matthew 12:9). They (presumably the Pharisees) asked, "Is it lawful to cure on the Sabbath?" Matthew adds: "so that they might accuse him." Jesus replies that it is lawful to do good on the Sabbath and heals not only the man but all who followed him (Matthew 7:12-15). Matthew adds that the Pharisees then took counsel against Jesus to put him to death.

The third encounter contains our passage. Jesus cures a blind and mute demoniac. The crowd was astounded and asked, "Could this perhaps be the Son of David?" The Pharisees heard this and retorted, "This man drives out demons only by the power of Beelzebul, the prince of demons" (Matthew 7:22-23). Jesus replies that if Satan drives out Satan, his kingdom cannot stand (Matthew 7:25-26) and later concludes, "Therefore, I say to you, every sin and blasphemy will be forgiven people, but blasphemy against the Spirit will not be forgiven. And whoever speaks a word against the Son of Man will be forgiven; but whoever speaks against the holy Spirit will not be forgiven, either in this age or in the age to come" (Matthew 7:31-32).

All three encounters surround Jesus performing corporal works of mercy: feeding the hungry, healing the sick, and casting out demons (free the imprisoned). The Pharisees rejected the first two as a violation of God's Law and the third as the work of the devil.

With these things in mind, let's answer our two questions.

Why can blasphemy against Jesus be potentially forgiven? St. John Chrysostom answers by noting that blaspheming the Son of Man may be due to ignorance, which can be corrected and receive forgiveness. Why, then, is the speaking against the Holy Spirit unforgivable? Because such blasphemy is due not to ignorance, but an outright rejection of God's acts of mercy.

But why is it unforgivable? Is it too great of a sin? 1 John 1:9 says, "If we acknowledge our sins, he is faithful and just and will forgive our sins …". If one comes to the point where he can look at God's loving mercy and call it demonic, that person will never be able to acknowledge their sins because they'll never see them as sins. They have come to the point of final impenitence, the refusal to repent by the end of one's life. As the Catechism explains, "There are no limits to the mercy of God, but anyone who deliberately refuses to accept his mercy by repenting, rejects the forgiveness of his sins and the salvation offered by the Holy Spirit …" (CCC 1864).

Matthew 4:15-16 - Finding Peter's House (August 8, 2016)

A big part of Jesus' public ministry took place in a small village named Capernaum. Located on the western shore of the Sea of

Galilee near a highway that spanned from the Mediterranean coast to Damascus, it was considered a frontier town with a small garrison of soldiers and a customs post.

The prophet Isaiah prophetically singled out this region as the place where the misfortunes that had visited Old Testament Israel would be reversed. The Assyrian invasions that decimated the northern tribes of Israel from 733 to 732 B.C. began in the region of Galilee (2 Kings 15:29). Therefore, Isaiah foretold that God's restoration would begin where these misfortunes started:

"O land of Zabulon, land of Nephthalim, and the rest inhabiting the sea-coast, and the land beyond Jordan, Galilee of the Gentiles. O people walking in darkness, behold a great light: you that dwell in the region and shadow of death, a light shall shine upon you" (Isaiah 9:1-2 LXX).

Jesus fulfilled this passage when he left Nazareth to live in Capernaum (Matthew 4:15-16). He is the great light that was manifested to the gentiles through his teaching and numerous miracles and healings. Think about it. It was in or around Capernaum that Jesus healed Jairus' daughter (Matt 9:18–26; Mark 5:21–43; Luke 8:41–56) and the woman with the issue of blood (Mark 5:21-43). He freed the possessed man (Mark 1:21–28) and healed the paralytic (Matt 9:2–8; Mark 2:1–12; Luke 5:17–20). He also called Peter and Andrew to become "fishers of men" (Matt 4:19; Mark 1:17) and later visited Peter's house in Capernaum to heal Peter's mother-in-law (Matt 8:14, Mark 1:29-31). It also was at the synagogue in Capernaum that Jesus delivered the Bread of Life discourse (John 6:59).

Capernaum today offers two remarkable archeological finds. First, one of the oldest synagogues in the world was found in Capernaum, dating from the fourth or fifth century A.D. What's interesting about this synagogue is that underneath its foundation is an older basalt foundation. It appears that the synagogue had been built upon the remains of an older one and might have used some of its stones for its edifice. If this is so, the older synagogue could very well be the place where Jesus delivered the Bread of Life discourse.

Another fascinating discovery was made not far from this ancient synagogue: In 1921, a small ancient Christian church was discovered dating from the fifth century A.D. From the writings of a pilgrim around A.D. 570, it is believed that this church could be the house of St. Peter himself. But how could a fifth century church be the location of Peter's house?

In 1968, further excavations revealed that underneath the church lay the ruins of a first century house with a few small rooms clustered around a courtyard. One room in particular caught the attention of the excavators: it had been renovated into a meeting place. Its walls were plastered from floor to ceiling, a very unusual feature for this time, and it contained large storage jars and oil lamps. Various inscriptions in Greek and Hebrew were found on its walls, saying things like, "Lord Jesus Christ help your servant" and "Christ have mercy" along with small crosses and even a boat.

What made this room so important that it was renovated and transformed into a first century house-church? Given that a fifth century church associated with Peter's house was built directly above this special room, it's not hard to figure out its significance. It appears that this was Peter's house where Jesus visited and healed

Peter's mother-in-law. It became a location where the earliest Christians worshipped, and when the house had fallen into disrepair, a new church was built directly above it. Christians continued to venerate this site up until the fifth and sixth centuries, when it, too, had fallen into ruins.

The care that the earliest Christians showed in venerated and preserving this location should give us confidence in our faith, since we have no doubt that the same care was used to pass on the faith that was once for all handed on to the saints (Jude 3).

Matthew 6:12 (Luke 11:4) - The Economics of Sin (July 14, 2017)

The most famous prayer in Christianity has to be the "Our Father." We all know it by heart. But if you compare the Our Father we pray with Matthew 6:12 (Luke 11:4) you'll notice that the words are somewhat different. We commonly pray "forgive us our trespasses as we forgive those who trespass against us," but the text itself speaks of debts. Matthew 6:12 says, "…and forgive us our debts (Greek, *opheiletēs*; Latin, *debita*), as we forgive our debtors" and Luke 11:4 says, "… and forgive us our sins for we ourselves forgive everyone in debt to us…" Trespasses, I understand. But what is all this about debts? There is something more going on here than meets the eye.

There are a few instances in the Old Testament where Scripture regards sin and righteous deeds as debts and credits. For example, when King Nebuchadnezzar revealed his dream about being under God's judgment, the prophet Daniel replied:

> "Therefore, O king, take my advice; atone [Redeem] for your sins by good deeds, and for your misdeeds by kindness to the poor; then your prosperity will be long" (Daniel 4:24).

The word "redeem" is commonly used in the Bible for money that is paid to free someone from slavery (Leviticus 25:47-49). Nebuchadnezzar's sins had placed him in debt to God, and good deeds (almsgiving) pays the debt back.

In the New Testament, Our Lord uses the analogy of debt in the parable of the unmerciful servant (Matthew 18:23-35). The King (the Father) forgives a servant of a massive debt. However, when that servant runs into another person who owes him a smaller debt, he demands repayment. The King learns of what had happened and calls back the unmerciful servant and demands that he pay back his entire debt. Jesus concludes: "So will my heavenly Father do to you, unless each of you forgives his brother from his heart."

Where sin is likened to a debt, good deeds (especially giving to the poor) are likened to credit. The Book of Proverbs teaches us:

> "He who has compassion on the poor lends to the LORD, and he will repay him for his good deed" (Proverbs 19:17).

In this rather shocking verse, we learn that in giving to the poor, we become God's creditor. St. Basil, commenting on this verse, says:

> "Consider the force of the statement, and you will admire the kindness of the Lawmaker. Whenever you have the intention of providing for a poor man for the Lord's sake, the same thing is both a

> gift and a loan, a gift because of the expectation of no repayment, but a loan because of the great gift of the Master who pays in his place, and who, receiving trifling things through a poor man, will give great things in return for them. 'He that hath mercy on the poor, lendeth to God.'"

The New Testament likewise speaks of righteous deeds in terms of credit. For example, our Lord speaks of giving to the poor in terms of accumulating a heavenly treasure when he speaks to the rich man in Matthew 19:21. Jesus tells the rich man, "... If you wish to be perfect, go, sell what you have and give to (the) poor, and you will have treasure in heaven. Then come, follow me." In regards to fasting and almsgiving, Jesus says, "Do not store up for yourselves treasures on earth ... But store up treasures in heaven ... For where your treasure is, there also will your heart be" (Matthew 6:19-21).

All of this should be kept in its proper perspective. Every good work is the product of God's grace that we freely assent to do. Therefore, the debt that is repaid through almsgiving is God's grace working in us. Likewise, the righteous deeds that we do are also done freely by God's grace. Therefore, whether it be our works of repentance for sin or the good deeds that we do, it is all grace working in us. As the Catechism of the Catholic Church says, quoting St. Augustine, "You are glorified in the assembly of your Holy Ones, for in crowning their merits you are crowning your own gifts" (CCC 2006).

Matthew 9:20-21 - The Truth About Tassels: Healing Those On The Fringe (November 23, 2016)

Handwriting can be laborious. Generally, if something is going to be written down, it needs to be important to the narrative. Otherwise, it's just extra work. It's for this reason that sometimes even small, incidental details in the Gospels can be very significant.

Take, for example, how Matthew recounts the healing of the woman with hemorrhages. He simply notes that a "… woman suffering hemorrhages for twelve years came up behind him and touched the tassel on his cloak. She said to herself, 'If only I can touch his cloak, I shall be cured'" (Matthew 9:20-21). Jesus recognizes what has happened and responds, "Courage, daughter! Your faith has saved you" and the woman was cured.

As you can see, Matthew's description is pretty bare bones except for one detail that doesn't seem to have any bearing on the episode: Jesus' tassels. Wait a second! Tassels? Why did Jesus' garment have tassels? Jesus was an observant Jew, and the Law of Moses said that the Israelites should put tassels on the corners of their garments:

> "The LORD said to Moses, 'Speak to the Israelites and tell them that they and their descendants must put tassels on the corners of their garments, fastening each corner tassel with a violet cord. When you use these tassels, let the sight of them remind you to keep all the commandments of the LORD, without going wantonly astray after the desires of your hearts and eyes. Thus you will remember to keep all my commandments and be holy to your God" (Number 15:37-39).

These tassels were affixed to the four corners of the garment by a cord. Their function was to be a tangible reminder for the Jews to keep God's commandments and be holy. Catholics and Orthodox also use religious objects for a similar purpose: namely, to inspire devotion to God and the desire to live a holy life. Jesus embraced this commandment to wear tassels, even though he castigated the Pharisees for "lengthening their tassels" out of pride (Matthew 23:5-6).

But why was it significant that the woman wished to touch Jesus' tassels, as opposed to touching some other garment? The answer may be found in Zechariah 8:20-23, where it is prophesied:

> "… There shall yet come peoples, the inhabitants of many cities; and the inhabitants of one city shall approach those of another, and say, 'Come! let us go to implore the favor of the LORD'; and, 'I too will go to seek the LORD.' … In those days ten men of every nationality, speaking different tongues, shall take hold, yes, take hold of every Jew by the edge of his garment [literally, "tassels"] and say, 'Let us go with you, for we have heard that God is with you.'"

The woman with the hemorrhages wasn't alone. Later in Matthew we find that:

> "When the men of that place recognized him [Jesus], they sent word to all the surrounding country. People brought to him all those who were sick and begged him that they might touch only the tassel on his cloak, and as many as touched it were healed" (Matthew 14:35-36).

Zechariah saw that one day those on the fringe of Jewish society (i.e., gentiles) would come and implore "the favor of the Lord" by grabbing on to every Jew's tassel. The gentiles wishing to touch only the tassel on Jesus' garment certain evokes Zechariah's thoughts.

It's important to also note that Jesus not only approved of using physical objects to remind us to live a holy life, but also that he was very comfortable using material things to affect spiritual benefits. There are dozens of examples in the New Testament where Jesus and his apostles heal using some physical medium such as by touching (Matthew 20:31-34), by smearing mud (John 9:6), and even by face cloths and aprons that had contact with the apostles (Acts 9:11-12). The same is true for the sacraments of the Church where God uses physical things (i.e., water, bread, wine, oil, etc.) as visible signs of invisible graces.

Matthew 16:18 - "You are Peter...": The Rocky Background to Jesus' words (October 5, 2015)

Last week, the papacy was front and center as Pope Francis made his first visit to the United States and Cuba. For me, whenever I see the pope, my mind races back to one passage: Matthew 16:18, in which Jesus gives Simon the name "rock" (Peter) and says that upon "this rock I will build my Church." It is here that Simon Peter receives Christ's promise that he will be the foundation of the Church.

Because this passage speaks directly to the authority of the pope, being the bishop of Rome and successor to the Apostle Peter, more ink has been spilled over this passage than perhaps any other in the New Testament.

While all the fireworks surround Christ's words and their meaning, a seemingly unimportant verse has largely gone unnoticed, at least by the average Joe Catholic in the pew. That verse is verse 13: "When Jesus went into the region of Caesarea Philippi he asked his disciples, 'Who do people say that the Son of Man is?'" To us, the location of Jesus' words to his disciples doesn't seem important. What's so interesting about Caesarea Philippi? Quite a bit, actually.

Caesarea Philippi is located along the southern slopes of Mount Hermon. It was originally called Panion because its pagan inhabitants worshiped the Greek god Pan within the caves and niches of the area. Panion also was known for a cave that had within it a very deep spring that once fed the river Jordan. After King Herod the Great received the town from Caesar Augustus, he built a beautiful white temple at the top of the hill dedicated to Caesar. When Herod died, his son Philip renamed the town Caesarea in the emperor's honor. Hence, the town became known as Caesarea Philippi. It is here, amidst this rocky terrain, that Jesus renames Simon Peter.

The location provides an interesting backdrop and contrast to Our Lord's words. Where the wicked King Herod the Great had built a pagan temple atop a huge outcrop of rock dedicated to a pagan emperor, Jesus (the true King of Israel) has established His rock (Simon Peter) upon which He built the true Church dedicated to the true God.

Where the rocky hills of Caesarea Philippi could not prevent the rushing water from the deep from flowing out, the "gates of the hades" will not prevail against Christ's rock, Simon Peter. Jesus speaks about His Church, a rock, and the powers of the underworld in sight of a false temple, a rock, and the waters of the deep. Coincidence? I think not.

Another layer of meaning can be seen in the niches and shrines that were dug into the rock wall at Caesarea Philippi. These niches served as shrines to worship the god Pan. For those who aren't up on Greek mythology, Pan was known for a lot of things. He was said to dwell in the desert and to cause confusion among travelers (i.e., we get the word "panic" from the Greek word *panikos*, which means "fear of Pan"). He's also associated with music; perhaps you've heard of "pan pipes" or "pan flutes." But Pan was mostly known as the god of flocks and shepherds. This ascription is particularly striking, given how Christ will bestow his promises to Simon Peter elsewhere in John 21:15-17. In this passage, Jesus appears to the apostles after His resurrection; he calls them and they recognize him. Speaking to Simon Peter, Christ asks three times, "Do you love me?" and responds with "Feed my lambs," "Tend my sheep," and "Feed my sheep," making Peter the shepherd of Christ's flock.

Unlike Pan, a false god of flocks and shepherds, Christ is the true God and Shepherd who commissions Peter to feed and tend His flock

Matthew 16:19 - The Key to Understanding the Papacy (Sept. 5, 2014)

Did you ever notice how the papacy is associated with keys? The Vatican flag has keys on it. Statues of St. Peter have him holding a set of keys. What is this association with St. Peter and the keys? Is it biblical? What does it tell us about Peter and the papacy?

The image comes from a very important passage in the New Testament, Matthew 16:18-19, where Jesus gives Simon the name Peter (meaning "rock") and says to Peter "I will give you the keys to the kingdom of heaven. Whatever you bind on earth shall be bound in heaven; and whatever you loose on earth shall be loosed in heaven." Jesus promised that he will give Simon Peter the "keys of the kingdom." What are the keys of the kingdom?

To us today, the keys of the kingdom reference would be easy to miss. After all, there aren't many functioning kingdoms in the world and those that do may not use this symbol. However, the "keys of the kingdom" was something well known in Jesus' day since all ancient middle-eastern monarchies shared a similar structure.

The king was the head of the kingdom, the highest authority for the state. Underneath the king were various offices of ministry. For example, the Kingdom of David's cabinet ministers included the head of the army, chief of the commissaries, superintendent of the labor force, etc. (see 1 Kings 4:1-6). Over these offices was the office of prime minister (sometimes call the master of the palace or the major domo). The prime minister's job was to oversee the other ministers and to look after the day-to-day operation of the kingdom. A king could not be bothered with micromanaging the kingdom's daily affairs, his concern was the micromanagement of the kingdom, such as long and short term planning, treatises and alliances, etc.. The micromanagement of the kingdom was given to the prime minister, whose authority was second only to the king.

We catch a glimpse of this office in the Isaiah 22 when a wicked prime minister, Shebna, was removed and replaced more worthy servant named Eliakim. God says to Shebna through Isaiah:

"On that day I will summon my servant Eliakim, son of Hilkiah; I will clothe him with your robe, and gird him with your sash, and give over to him your authority. He shall be a father to the inhabitants of Jerusalem, and to the house of Judah. I will place the key of the House of David on his shoulder; when he opens, no one shall shut, when he shuts, no one shall open."

Among the signs of the prime minister's office (a robe, a sash, the title "father") was the "key of the House of David," that is to say the keys of the kingdom. The prime minister wore this large key on his shoulder and used it to open and shut the gates of the kingdom.

Therefore, when Christ promised Simon Peter the "keys of the Kingdom," the Apostles must have realized two things by this action: First, they must have realized that by doing this Christ was acting as the son of David, the King of Messiah king, whose kingdom extends to both heaven and earth. Second, Jesus promised to install Simon Peter as the prime minister of this kingdom. His job, therefore, would be to oversee the other ministers in the kingdom (i.e., the Apostles) in their ministry. And just as the office of prime minister in the Davidic kingdom didn't end when someone died or was removed from office, neither did Peter's office end when St. Peter died in Rome sometime around AD 68. Rather, the office continued and the authority of the keys continues through St. Peter's successors, the Pope, with Pope Francis being the 267th person to occupy this office and exercise the power of the keys.

Matthew 16:19 - No Need to Get Tied Up with "Binding and Loosing" (August 20, 2015)

More ink has been spilled by scholars on Matthew 16:16-19 than perhaps any other passage in the New Testament, and for good reason. It is the passage in which Jesus makes Simon the "rock" upon which He will build His future Church, thus making it a good proof for the primacy of the pope, the successor to the chair of Peter.

In previous articles, we looked at the biblical background behind Simon's name change and the "keys of the kingdom of heaven." We haven't looked, however, at an oft-ignored but equally illuminating proof text in the same passage, namely, the bestowal of the power to "bind and loose."

In Matthew 16:19, Jesus says to Simon Peter, "I will give you the keys to the kingdom of heaven. Whatever you bind on earth shall be bound in heaven; and whatever you loose on earth shall be loosed in heaven."

What does "bind" and "loose" mean? These terms come, not from the Old Testament, but from the synagogue. Binding and loosing are rabbinical terms that mean the power to place the community under obligation (i.e., "to bind") or the release the community from an obligation (i.e., "to loose"). The terms equally apply to doctrinal matters (e.g., declaring what is true doctrine) as well as to disciplinary decisions (e.g., banishing someone from the community or allowing them back).

By applying these terms to Simon Peter, Jesus is investing him with jurisdictional authority over His Church. More than that, Peter's authority to bind and loose is sanctioned from heaven. Whatever Peter binds on earth *shall be bound in heaven,* and whatever he looses on earth *shall be loosed in heaven.*

The Jewish background to these words also singles out the uniqueness of the authority given to Peter. During the time of Jesus, the pastoral care for the Jewish people centered on the local synagogue. The rabbi had authority to bind and loose local decisions. However, there was a higher, broader authority, which was known as the Great Bet Din (or "House of Judgment").

According to the *JPS Guide to Jewish Tradition,* "...the Great Sanhedrin exercised sweeping judicial, legislative, and executive powers and was the only court that could try 'a tribe, a false prophet, and a *Kohen Gadol* (High Priest)' (Sanh. 1:5)..." Although local rabbis had the power to bind and loose, the president of the Great Bet Din alone had the ultimate authority to bind and loose in matters of doctrine and disciple.

If Judah the Prince (R. Yahudah ha-nasi), a rabbi who lived in the second century A.D., tells us anything about the role of the "president" of the Great Bet Din, he shows us that the president was more than an administrator. He was a patriarchal figure who could create new law by personal decree. In fact, Judah the Prince is accredited with finalizing the Jewish oral law known as the Mishnah.

Given this background, it seems likely that Jesus' promise of the "keys of the kingdom" and the power to bind and loose makes Simon Peter both the prime minister of Christ's kingdom and the president over the Christian community, respectively, since both were associated with the special prerogatives of these officers.

A common rejoinder against any special authority given to Peter is that Jesus also gives the power to bind and loose to the rest of the apostles in Matthew 18:18, so Peter receives nothing special. The problem with this is that Simon Peter actually receives this power twice, once in Matthew 16:19 and again in Matthew 18:18. Why?

I believe the different contexts in both passages offer us a solution. In Matthew 16, Jesus is talking about "*my* Church" — that is, the Church as a whole. In Matthew 18:15-18, Jesus is addressing the reconciliation of a sinner with a local Church, where the local bishop would have jurisdiction. If this is correct, then Jesus giving the same authority twice makes sense, because the pope has jurisdiction over the whole Church, and he is also the bishop of Rome. He has universal jurisdiction and local jurisdiction, where the rest of the Apostles (and their successors) would have only local jurisdiction.

Matthew 21:11 - What's So Great About Galilee? (July 28, 2017)

If you're reading the Gospel according to Matthew, you might have noticed he highlights the fact that Jesus spent a lot of time in Galilee.

When the crowds in Jerusalem noticed the tumult of Jesus' arrival, they asked, "Who is this?" The crowd didn't say "Jesus of Nazareth," but "Jesus the prophet, from Nazareth in Galilee" (Matthew 21:11). Why note that Nazareth is in Galilee? Moreover, after St. Joseph was informed by an angel in a dream that it was OK to bring Mary and Jesus back to Israel after Herod's death, where did Joseph go? Galilee. Matthew also notes that Jesus left Galilee to go meet John the Baptist (Matthew 3:13) and he returned there after John's arrest (Matthew 4:12). Galilee is where Jesus calls the apostles (Matthew 4:18). Jesus' disciples were also told that after Jesus was raised up, he would meet them in Galilee (Matthew 26:32, 28:7). Galilee, Galilee, Galilee! What's so big about Galilee?

Galilee happens to be a very important place in salvation history. King David's kingdom was comprised of all of the 12 tribes of Israel, but not long afterward his kingdom became divided. Two tribes in the south remained faithful to David's kingdom (Judah and Benjamin). The other 10 tribes, located in the north, broke off and formed their own kingdom. These 10 tribes disappear from history after the Assyrians invade the north and take these tribes away into captivity. Galilee is mentioned as one of the last cities to be taken by the Assyrians (2 Kings 15:29).

The prophets, especially Isaiah and Jeremiah, spoke of God one day restoring David's kingdom and gathering back into one the lost tribes of Israel. Where would this ingathering begin? You guessed it. Galilee. God says through Jeremiah, "Set up road markers, put up guideposts; Turn your attention to the highway, the road by which you went. Turn back, O virgin Israel, turn back to these your cities" (Jeremiah 31:21). The road to exile was from Galilee.

Jeremiah also says, "Behold, I will bring them back from the land of the north; I will gather them from the ends of the world, with the blind and the lame in their midst, The mothers and those with child; they shall return as an immense throng" (Jeremiah 31:8). Is it any wonder that it was while Jesus heals the blind and the lame while in Galilee! "He went around all of Galilee, teaching in their synagogues, proclaiming the gospel of the kingdom, and curing every disease and illness among the people" (Matthew 4:23).

Later in Matthew, Jesus was walking by the Sea of Galilee and "(g)reat crowds came to him, having with them the lame, the blind, the deformed, the mute, and many others. They placed them at his feet, and he cured them. The crowds were amazed when they saw the mute speaking, the deformed made whole, the lame walking, and the blind able to see, and they glorified the God of Israel" (Matthew 15:30-31).

Isaiah also prophesied about Galilee. In fact, Matthew quotes Isaiah as saying, "'Land of Zebulun and land of Naphtali, the way to the sea, beyond the Jordan, Galilee of the Gentiles, the people who sit in darkness have seen a great light, on those dwelling in a land overshadowed by death light has arisen'" (Matthew 4:13-16 quoting Isaiah 9:1-2). Galilee did see a great light. First, they enjoyed the light of the Gospel that Jesus taught. Second, the blind and the lame were restored to heath. Third, Galilee was the location of Jesus' first appearance after the resurrection (Matthew 28:16-17).

It's interesting that only Matthew records Jesus' first appearance in Galilee; Mark and Luke skip over it. John records another appearance in Galilee when Jesus appoints Peter the shepherd of his sheep (John 21). The "great light" that those of Galilee saw was the resurrected Messiah. God had changed the place of Israel's most bitter punishment into the place of Israel's great joy, the restoration of the Messiah King.

Matthew 22:24-29 (also, Mark 12:18-29 and Luke 20:27-40) - An Odd Challenge: Seven Marriages to Seven Brothers (March 6, 2015)

No, the title isn't a misprint. Rather, it is a reference to a challenge that the Sadducees put to Jesus in Matthew 22:24-29 (also, Mark 12:18-29 and Luke 20:27-40):

"Teacher, Moses said, 'If a man dies without children, his brother shall marry his wife and raise up descendants for his brother.' Now there were seven brothers among us. The first married and died and, having no descendants, left his wife to his brother. The same happened with the second and the third, through all seven. Finally the woman died. Now at the resurrection, of the seven, whose wife will she be? For they all had been married to her.'"

Why did the Sadducees question the resurrection, and why did they use such a bizarre scenario to prove their point? A peak at what's going on behind the Bible clues us in on one possible motive.

Why did the Sadducees question the resurrection? Acts 23:7-8 tells us that this Jewish sect not only did not believe in the resurrection, but they didn't believe in angels, either. Why didn't they believe in these things? The fathers of the Church taught that the Sadducees accepted only the first five books of the Bible, the books of Moses. Because the resurrection (and angels) are more explicitly taught in the later books of the Old Testament, they rejected these teachings.

But why propose such an odd scenario as a woman remaining childless through seven marriages to her husband's brothers? Isn't that odd? To us, yes, it is very strange. But according to the Old Testament law, if a woman marries and her husband dies without producing a child, it was the duty of the man's brother to marry her and produce an offspring for him (Deuteronomy 25:5, Genesis 38:8).

The Sadducees were attempting to pit the resurrection against the law of Moses. Because Moses commanded that the brother(s) should raise up an offspring, who would be the woman's husband at the Resurrection?

But the problem still remains: Why use such an outlandish scenario to prove your point? If you think about it, two marriages to two brothers would have proved it just as well. By proposing seven childless marriages to seven brothers, the Sadducees' challenge could easily have backfired. All Jesus would have to say is: "Show me such a thing and I'll answer your question."

My suspicion is that there is more going on behind this text than meets the eye; in fact, there is a biblical example of a woman remaining childless after seven marriages to seven brothers. It takes place in the Book of Tobit (Tobit 3:8, 15).

Could the Sadducees be harkening to Tobit? If they did, it would add a new dimension to their argument. Remember, the Sadducees only accepted the first five books of the Bible. They didn't accept Tobit as Scripture, but Jesus did. Why, then, use this example?

Perhaps it was to force Jesus' hand, not only on the resurrection, but also on Tobit. Had Our Lord said, "Show me such a woman and I'll answer your question," they would have said, "See, your book of Tobit said this happened." Jesus would then either be forced to dismisses Tobit (and possibly discredit himself in the eyes of His followers) or admit the problem is unanswerable and makes the resurrection seem absurd.

Jesus, of course, does neither. He says to the Sadducees, "You are misled because you do not know the scriptures or the power of God. At the resurrection they neither marry nor are given in marriage, but are like the angels in heaven" (Matthew 22:29-30).

Our Lord then goes on offense, citing a passage from the books of Moses (Exodus 3:6) that demonstrates the resurrection, saying "… have you not read what was said to you by God, 'I am the God of Abraham, the God of Isaac, and the God of Jacob'? He is not the God of the dead but of the living" (Matthew 22:31-32).

If this is so, the Sadducees may have had Tobit in their sights, as well as the resurrection.

Matthew 23:35 - Did John the Baptist's Father Die a Martyr? (September 2, 2016)

John the Baptist plays an important role in the Gospels as the one who was to prepare the way for the messiah. The Gospel of Luke provides for us information about John's parents, Zechariah and Elizabeth. John's father, Zechariah, was a priest who at the time of the incense offering in the Temple was visited by the angel Gabriel, who announced John's birth.

Zechariah didn't believe and could not talk until he witnessed John's birth and gave him his name (Luke 1:5-25, 57-80). The praise Zechariah offers at the birth of John is known as the *Benedictus* (Latin for "blessed"). This is the last we hear about Zechariah in Scripture, but this isn't the last we hear about him in Church history.

There was an early understanding in the Church that Zechariah died a martyr's death. When Jesus said to the scribes and Pharisees that "all the righteous bloodshed upon earth [will come upon you], from the righteous blood of Abel to the blood of Zechariah, the son of Barachiah, whom you murdered between the sanctuary and the altar," (Matthew 23:35) some early fathers believed Jesus was speaking about John the Baptist's father, Zechariah. Seeing that no other person mentioned in Scripture perfectly fits the description of this Zechariah, John's father is certainly a possible candidate.

Apocryphal writings that contain accounts about Zechariah's martyrdom in the temple area also circulated in the early Church. In fact, one of them, the Protoevangelium of James, was written sometime in the first quarter of the second Christian century, which is quite early since it is traditionally believed that St. John the Apostle died only a few decades earlier. According to this apocryphal writing, King Herod was searching for John the Baptist and sent guards to Zechariah to find out where he was. Zechariah replied that he is always in the temple area serving God and had no idea where John could be. When threatened with death, Zechariah is said to reply: "I am God's martyr, if you shed my blood; for the Lord will receive my spirit, because you shed innocent blood at the vestibule of the temple of the Lord." (Protoevangelium of James, 23). According to this story, the guards killed him and his body was found later on.

Another interesting story is given by the early Church father Gregory of Nyssa (d. AD 394). According this account, Zechariah, knowing about Mary's Virgin Birth of Christ, refused to remove Mary from praying in the place in the temple area reserved for virgins. When asked why he refused to remove Mary, Zechariah declared that "the King of creation, according to his divine pleasure, had come through a new kind of birth." Enraged, the crowd murdered Zechariah in front of the altar of sacrifice.

As you can see, the details in these sources differ quite a bit on the circumstances surrounding Zechariah's death. However, they do agree on two main points. First, they both attest that Zechariah, the father of John the Baptist, was martyred. Second, he was killed in the temple area.

Interestingly enough, archeology has also confirmed in this early Christian belief. In 2003, excavators in the Kidron valley discovered a fourth century inscription written on a monument called "Absalom's tomb" or "Absalom's pillar." The inscription reads, "This is the tomb of Zachariah, the martyr, the holy priest, the father of John." The inscription is too late to be a credible witness to the actual events, but it does show us that fourth century Christians believed Zechariah was a martyr.

If Zechariah was a martyr in the temple area, it does provide us with something to ponder. Remember, it was in the temple that Zechariah encountered the angel Gabriel, who gave the good news about John. Zechariah's response was less than stellar; he didn't believe and was struck dumb. Zechariah's death, according to these sources, shows us a complete reversal. Zechariah showed forth his belief in the temple area by attesting to the truth and through his martyrdom spoke out loudly about his faith.

Matthew 24:30, 32 - The End was Near? Scripture's Take on the Last Day (August 10, 2014)

Christians have long been fascinated about the "Last Things" — that is, what will take place at the end of time. If you're familiar with the subject, you may have noticed some passages seem to suggest that Christ and the New Testament authors believed the end was just around the corner.

For example, Jesus says in the Olivet Discourse, "And then the sign of the Son of Man will appear in heaven, and all the tribes of the earth will mourn, and they will see the Son of Man coming upon the clouds of heaven with power and great glory … Amen, I say to you, this generation will not pass away until all these things have taken place" (Matt 24:30, 34). And the book of Revelation begins by saying, "The revelation of Jesus Christ, which God gave to him, to show his servants what must happen soon …" (Rev 1:1).

Did the first Christians expect the world to end in their lifetime? The answer is no. They didn't expect the "end of the world" as much as the "end of the age." Their present age was to be replaced by the Messianic age (the "age to come"), and the destruction of the Jerusalem temple signaled that change.

The Olivet Discourse begins with the apostles admiring the temple and Jesus' prediction of its destruction (see Matt 24:1-3). This prediction was fulfilled when the pagan Romans destroyed the temple on Aug. 10, AD 70. Since the temple was the center for the sacrifices prescribed in the Old Testament, its destruction put a definitive end to the Old Covenant and ushered in the "age to come" where Jews and gentiles worshipped God through Christ's sacrifice on the cross, which fulfills all the sacrifices of the Old Covenant.

But if you look closer at these and other related passages, you'll notice they speak of the destruction of the temple and yet point beyond the temple to something greater. To understand why this is so, we need to dig a little deeper into the biblical background of the temple.

Some may be surprised to find that God was the first temple builder, as Scripture describes God's creation of the cosmos as one who is building a temple. For example, Psalm 78:69 says God, "…built his shrine [sanctuary] like the heavens, like the earth which he founded forever." God laid down a foundation (Job 9:6, 38:4-6, Psalm 18:15 [16], Heb 1:10). Like a wise master builder, He marked out and measured the cosmos (Job 38:4-11, Is 40:12) and raised its pillars (1 Sam 2:8, Job 9:6, 26:11, Psalm 75:4). The cosmos, therefore, is described as a temple written large — a macro-temple.

Conversely, the tabernacle built by Moses and especially Solomon's temple are presented as a miniature model of God's creation, a micro-cosmos. Scripture presents several interesting parallels that point to this connection. For example, God finished creation on the seventh day (Gen 2:2-3) and Solomon finished building the Jerusalem temple in seven years (1 Kings 6:38). Not only was the temple completed in seven years, but its dedication took place on the seventh month (1 Kings 8:2) and the feast of its inauguration lasted seven days (1 Kings 8:65)! God rested on the seventh day of creation and the temple is called "God's resting place forever" (Psalm 132:14). Even the builder of the temple, Solomon, harkens back to God's completion of creation since his name, Solomon, means "man of rest" or "man of peace." Dozens of other examples could be given, but this is enough to show that the temple was seen as a miniature model of God's creation.

This explains why the New Testament passages about the destruction of the temple also seem to point beyond the temple to the end of time. If the temple was a model of the cosmos, the destruction of the temple, in a mysterious way, models for us the consummation of creation, the end of time.

Matthew 26:61, Also Mark 14:58 - Sacred Ground: Is the body Really a Temple? (November 14, 2014)

When evidence was brought against Jesus by his accusers, one of them said, "This man said, 'I can destroy the temple of God and within three days rebuild it'" (Matthew 26:61, also Mark 14:58).

Their accusation was a distorted account of what Jesus actually said. When asked for a sign, Jesus replied, "Destroy this temple and in three days I will raise it up" (John 2:19). The Jews, like his accusers, thought that Our Lord was referring to the Jerusalem temple (John 2:20), but John tells us that Jesus "…was speaking about the temple of his body" (John 2:21). Where did our Lord and St. John get this idea of referring to a body as a temple? It came from the Bible, of course.

In fact, the Bible connects several ideas together with the body and temple. For example, Scripture sometimes refers to the temple or the tent of the tabernacle as a "house." Exodus 34:26 says that, "The choicest first fruits of your soil you shall bring to the house of the LORD, your God." Likewise, 1 Kings 9:10 says "After the twenty years during which Solomon built the two houses, the temple of the LORD and the palace of the king …"

The temple is one of the two "houses" built by Solomon. Jesus likewise taps into this association when he says (quoting Isaiah 56:7) to the moneychangers in the temple, "'My house shall be a house of prayer,' but you are making it a den of thieves" (Matthew 21:13, Mark 11:17, Luke 19:46). The temple can be likened to a house and elsewhere a house can refer to a body.

A really interesting house/body/temple connection is found in Second Samuel. King David lived in a palace, a house of cedar, and he thought it wrong for God to dwell in a tent (i.e., the tabernacle) so he decided he would build a temple for God (2 Samuel 7:2). In response to David's love for God, God said that it was not David who would build a house (temple), but that God would build a house for David: "Your house and your kingdom shall endure forever before me; your throne shall stand firm forever'" (2 Samuel

7:16). "House" here refers to David's bodily offspring, a royal dynasty. The temple is a house. David's bodily offspring (dynasty) is a house as well.

The same Hebrew association can be found in the writings of Paul. For example, Paul says in 2 Corinthians 5:1, "For we know that if the earthly tent which is our house is torn down, we have a building from God, a house not made with hands, eternal in the heavens." The "earthly tent" and "house" refers to our bodies. Likewise, Paul writes to the Corinthians, "Avoid immorality. Every other sin a person commits is outside the body, but the immoral person sins against his own body. Do you not know that your body is a temple of the Holy Spirit within you, whom you have from God, and that you are not your own?" (1 Corinthians 6:19-20). As you can see, Paul uses the words "tent," "house," "body," and "temple" interchangeably.

For the sake of completeness, we should also add the Church to this list. The Church is the body of Christ (Ephesians 5:23, Colossians 1:18, 24). It is therefore also a house: The Church is the "household of God, the pillar and foundation of truth" (1 Timothy 3:15) and we are "living stones" built into a "spiritual house" (1 Peter 2:5). This "spiritual house" is also described as a temple, "…a spiritual house to be a holy priesthood to offer spiritual sacrifices acceptable to God through Jesus Christ."

As you can see, there is more behind John's explanation of the temple referring to a body than first meets the eye. The next time you are reading Scripture and you see an association like this, dig a little deeper behind the meaning of the text. You might be surprised at what you'll find.

The Gospel According to Mark

The Preaching Gospel: Mark's Off-the-cuff Style (November 26, 2014)

Remember the old, "It is live, or is it Memorex" commercials? The idea was that this audio tape was so good that it sounded like a live performance. Every time I read Mark, I can't help but think of that commercial. Why? Mark doesn't read like a document that someone sat down to compose at a desk, but it reads more like a written record of a live speech. Consider this:

Very few people today handwrite letters or documents. Most of us compose our documents by typing them out on a word processor or some other device. The reason is simple: Handwriting takes a lot of time and can be hard work, especially if we have to write more than a few paragraphs. For that reason, authors (ancient and modern) when compositing handwritten documents always try to stick to the essentials. Adding extra side-comments, digressions and repetitions means more time and more work. Moreover, it doesn't necessarily help the reader understand the material.

Live speech, on the other hand, is a completely different animal. A public speaker has the advantage of instant feedback from his audience. It the audience seems puzzled by a point, the speaker can add a few side comments, make a digression, or repeat whatever is needed to hit the point home. Unlike a composition at a desk, additional material is essential to live speaking, and this is exactly what we find in the Gospel of Mark.

Let's highlight a few of these features. In Mark 7, the Gospel recounts the Pharisees objecting to Christ's disciples eating without ritually washing their hands. Perhaps sensing that his audience was baffled by this objection, the text digresses and explains a little more about ritual cleanness, "(For the Pharisees and, in fact, all Jews, do not eat without carefully washing their hands, keeping the tradition of the elders. And on coming from the marketplace they do not eat without purifying themselves. And there are many other things that they have traditionally observed, the purification of cups and jugs and kettles (and beds))" (Mark 7:3-4). A good editor would never let this leave his desk. He would have re-written the passage incorporating these comments so that it read seamlessly. But just like one who was delivering this message to a live audience, Mark adds it as an additional comment to clarify things. Again, a speaker would do this, not an author.

There is a similar example with the widow donating two small coins to the temple (Mark 12:41). The text says she gave two "lepta," which is a Palestinian nickname for the coins, meaning literally, "tiny." When recounting this incident, Mark says she gave two "tiny" to the temple. After stating this, he quickly adds that they are two quadrans (i.e., the smallest denomination of Roman coinage). Again, an editor would replace "lepta" with "quadrans," but the clarification is tacked on to the end, like one would do in a live speech.

Those who have read Mark would immediately recognize this last example: His use of the word "immediately." In its 16 short chapters, Mark uses the word "immediately" 41 times! In grade school, when the teacher made us write out a word 40 times, it would be looked upon as a punishment. Likewise, if you were to handwrite a lengthy book, such repetition would be something to avoid. However, a speaker would naturally use such devices to try to inject some excitement into his discourse.

There are many other telltale signs of a live discourse in Mark, so the next time you read this Gospel, keep this background in mind. You might be surprised what else you'll find.

Mark 1:1-4 - The Mysterious John the Baptist (February 5, 2016)

Not many things make it into all four Gospels. In fact, the Gospel of John usually includes material that isn't found in Matthew, Mark or Luke. John the Baptist happens to be one person who is mentioned in all four, and yet despite this coverage, we still don't know a lot about this mysterious figure. This is where looking "behind the Bible" may help fill in our picture of John.

In the 1940s, we found the Dead Sea Scrolls in the desert caves in Qumran. These scrolls were the writings of a Jewish desert community that flourished during Jesus' lifetime. Scholars have noted several intriguing parallels between John the Baptist and the Qumran community. For example, both practiced asceticism and separated themselves from Jerusalem. John's unusual diet of locust and honey would have been allowed at Qumran.

Qumran was also a priestly community, and John came from a priestly family. Both emphasized ritual washings and saw the desert as a place of preparation. Even more intriguing, John's journey into the desert took place only a few miles from Qumran. Was John part of the Qumran community? As tantalizing as these parallels are, we really don't know. They're not definitive.

Another extra-biblical source that sheds light on John is the first century Jewish historian, Josephus, who wrote the following about John:

"[John the Baptist]... was a good man, and commanded the Jews to exercise virtue, both as to righteousness towards one another, and piety towards God, and so to come to baptism ... Now, when [many] others came in crowds about him, for they were greatly moved [or pleased] by hearing his words, Herod, who feared lest the great influence John had over the people might put it into his power and inclination to raise a rebellion (for they seemed ready to do anything he should advise), thought it best, by putting him to death, to prevent any mischief he might cause, and not bring himself into difficulties, by sparing a man who might make him repent of it when it should be too late.

"Accordingly he was sent a prisoner, out of Herod's suspicious temper, to Macherus, the castle I before mentioned, and was there put to death. Now the Jews had an opinion that the destruction of this army was sent as a punishment upon Herod, and a mark of God's displeasure against him" (*Antiquities*, 18, 116-119).

Josephus and the Gospels dovetail nicely because they both look at John's death from two different perspectives. The Gospels recount John's death from John's perspective. John preached that Herod Antipas' marriage to Herodias, his half-brother's wife, was unlawful (Mark 6:18). Leviticus forbids such marriages while the brother is still alive (Leviticus 18:16, 20:21). The Gospels tells us that Herod did not kill John because he feared the crowds who knew John to be a righteous man (Mark 6:19-20).

Josephus looks at the same event from a political angle. Herod feared that John had too much influence over his followers and so he killed him before any trouble could start. But Josephus' account alone doesn't make sense. It's not good policy to kill off people of good reputation just because they're popular or influential. Herod had to have seen John as a personal threat, and that is exactly what the Gospels supply. John was preaching against Herod's marriage, and because (as Josephus notes) John had an enormous influence over his followers because of his righteousness, Herod had to stop John before the crowd turned on him. Herodias' prompting sealed John's fate.

Both the Gospels and Josephus have an important lesson to teach us about holiness. John had nothing. He was poor. He didn't have luxurious clothing or live in a royal palace like Herod (Matthew 11:8, Luke 7:25-26), yet even the mighty Herod Antipas feared him. Why? Because he lived fully and faithfully to God's will, even to the point of speaking out publically against unrighteous actions.

The crowds followed John because of his spiritual integrity. He followed God both in and out of season. For this reason, John the Baptist's life is praised throughout history in the four Gospels and even by Josephus.

Mark 4:1-11 - Christ's Fast in the Desert is an Answer to Israel's History (March 24, 2017)

When God became man and dwelt among us, everything He did was revelatory and packed with meaning. But sometimes it is not always clear why Jesus did the things he did. For example, why did Jesus go into the desert for 40 days fasting, praying, and being tested by the devil (Matthew 4:1-11, Mark 1:12-13, Luke 4:1-13)? A few Old Testament texts might shed light as to why.

The two most prominent persons in the Old Testament and in the Jewish faith are Moses and Elijah. Moses led the exodus (Israel's escape from slavery in Egypt), and it was through Moses that God gave his law or Torah to his people. Meanwhile, Elijah is perhaps one of the greatest of the Old Testament prophets; Sirach 48:4 says that none of the prophets can equal his glory. And if you recall, it was Moses and Elijah who had the honor of appearing with Jesus at the Transfiguration to talk with him about "the exodus" that he was to undergo (Luke 9:31).

What do Moses and Elijah have to do with Christ's fasting in the desert? Surprisingly, there is a tie-in: Both Old Testament figures also fasted for 40 days. After traveling through the desert, Moses and the people came to Mount Horeb:

"Then the LORD said to Moses, 'Write down these words, for in accordance with them I have made a covenant with you and with Israel.' So Moses stayed there with the LORD for forty days and forty nights, without eating any food or drinking any water, and he wrote on the tablets the words of the covenant, the ten commandments" (Exodus 34:27-28).

Elijah also made a 40-day fast when he fled for his life into the desert. An angel appeared to him and gave bread and water to sustain him on his journey. 1 Kings 19:8 says, "He got up, ate and drank; then strengthened by that food, he walked forty days and forty nights to the mountain of God, Horeb" (1 Kings 19:8).

When we look at both figures through the wider lens of the exodus, we see several parallels. In the exodus, Moses and the Israelites escaped slavery in Egypt by passing through the water of the Red Sea and fleeing into the desert. In the desert, the Israelites murmured against Moses because they had nothing to eat or drink, so God sent them bread (manna) and water (from a rock). An angel provided Elijah with food and God provided the manna, which is called "the food of angels" (Wisdom 16:20). Moses, Elijah, and the Israelites walk through the desert to Mount Horeb (sometimes called Sinai). Moses and Elijah fasted for 40 days. Israel was in the desert for 40 years.

Looking at Christ's life as outlined in Matthew's Gospel, we see an interesting pattern. After King Herod died, the holy family, who were hiding in Egypt, return, thus fulfilling the Scripture "Out of Egypt I called my son" (Matthew 2:15, Hosea 11:1). But what's interesting is that Hosea wasn't speaking directly about the messiah; he was speaking about the exodus.

The Israelites passed through water after leaving Egypt, and Jesus passes through water at his baptism (Matthew 3). Next, Jesus is led by the Spirit into the desert and fasts for 40 days, just as Israel was led by God into the desert and remained there for 40 years.

Unlike Israel, who tested God by their disobedience, the devil tests Jesus' obedience. Three times he approaches our Lord and Jesus responds with three quotes from the book of Deuteronomy. Each quote is important. The first quote is a reply to Israel's complaint about hunger (Deuteronomy 8:3). The second is a response to the complaint about being thirsty (Deuteronomy 6:16, Exodus 17:1) and the last (Deuteronomy 6:12 or 10:20) recounts the whole episode of the exodus. In other words, where Israel failed during the time of testing in the desert, Jesus succeeds by recounting the words that Israel should have said.

Jesus' life seems to be repeating or recapitulating Israel's experience in the exodus. This Lent, let's join Jesus in being faithful during our trials.

Mark 3:14 - The Holy Dozen: Why Twelve Apostles and Not Thirteen? (November 24, 2015)

Several years ago, I ran across a comment by a feminist theologian who stated that if Jesus had a 13th apostle, it would have been Mary Magdalene. What struck me as odd was its presupposition that the number of apostles was arbitrary, as if Jesus could have chosen 11 apostles or even 14. If you dig more into the background of the selection of the Twelve Apostles, some pretty important facts come to light.

The earliest and most obvious connection to the number twelve comes from the patriarch Jacob (also known as Israel). Jacob had twelve sons: Reuben, Simeon, Levi, Judah, Zebulon, Issachar, Dan, Gad, Asher, Naphtali, Joseph and Benjamin. These twelve individuals eventually formed the twelve tribes of Israel (Genesis 49:28).

What's interesting about this structure is that each of the twelve tribes was represented by a single individual, usually called a "ruler" (*nagid*) or a "prince" (*sar*) (1 Chronicles 27:16, 22 respectively). These rulers or princes were the elected leaders of each tribe, and each of the twelve rulers was in charge of their respective tribes. By the time David became king, the overall structure of the kingdom was quite complex, but still at the heart of it was the king and under him twelve ruler/princes who governed each of the twelve tribes.

So, the number twelve is quite predominant. Jacob had twelve sons, who became twelve tribes, who had elected twelve princes, who were ruled by one king.

This situation didn't last long. After David's son Solomon died, his successor Rehaboham refused to relieve the twelve tribes of the heavy tax burden left by Solomon's expansive government (1 Kings 12:1-19; 2 Chronicles 10:1-19) with the result that ten tribes broke off from David's kingdom and formed their own kingdom to the north, known as the Kingdom of Israel. This left only two tribes under the Davidic monarchy (Judah and Benjamin). This southern kingdom was known as the Kingdom of Judah.

To make a long story short, the sinfulness of both kingdoms led to disaster. The ten northern tribes were invaded by the Assyrians and taken into exile. Most of these Israelites were scattered, intermarried with the gentiles, and never return as a cohesive group. The two southern tribes of Judah were taken into exile by the Babylonians. Unlike the Kingdom of Israel, the southern tribes did return to their homeland, but they returned without a king.

God had promised David that his "house" (i.e., dynasty) would be everlasting, yet it appeared to have vanished along with the twelve tribes over which he ruled. The prophets reassured the people that this situation would not last forever. David's family tree might appear to be cut down, but God would raise up "… a shoot from the stump of Jesse" (Isaiah 11:1). Micah prophesied that he was to be born in Bethlehem and "when she who is to give birth has borne … the rest of his brethren shall return to the children of Israel." There would be a Davidic kingdom that would gather in the twelve tribes of Israel scattered throughout the world.

Jesus is the Messiah king, the true son of David, who after his birth in Bethlehem of the Blessed Virgin, "rebuilds the fallen tent of David" (Acts 15:16) and like a Good Shepherd gathers those who are lost back to himself. Just as King David ruled with twelve princes, Jesus chose twelve Apostles. But Christ's kingdom is more than David's earthly kingdom. It's not based on heredity or tied to one geographic location; it's based on grace. The Apostles are to teach, sanctify and govern all the people of God, regardless of their race. Like the twelve princes, the Apostles held offices which after their death were occupied by successors (bishops) who continued their ministry.

As such, the fact that there were twelve Apostles is very significant and certainly not arbitrary. They are the ones who, in the age to come, will sit on twelve thrones and judge the twelve tribes of Israel (Matthew 19:28, Luke 22:30). Twelve, in the Bible, means more than a dozen.

Mark 14:50-52 - The Naked Truth about the Young Man in Mark (Jan. 9, 2015)

The Gospels contain many vivid details of Christ's life, and some of them are very striking, if not odd. For example, did you ever wonder why Mark included the following details after Jesus was arrested?

Mark 14:50-52: "And they all left him and fled. Now a young man followed him wearing nothing but a linen cloth about his body. They seized him, but he left the cloth behind and ran off naked."

Why would Mark include this seemingly odd and inconsequential detail about the young man losing his clothing when his Gospel is only 16 chapters long? What is so profound about a young man running off without his clothes?

One could answer that Mark recorded it because it happened, which is certainly true, but it doesn't explain why he chose to include this detail and leave out dozens of others.

Another possible answer is that the "young man" was John Mark himself, and because it was personal he wished to include it in the Gospel. This is possible, but not very likely since the early Church fathers understood the young man to be either John the Apostle (Ambrose, Chrysostom) or James (Epiphanius). But even if the young man was John Mark, there must be more to the story than John Mark including a personal anecdote. Running off naked must have meant something more to his original audience.

I must confess I never gave this incident much thought until a good friend mine, Bob Salmon, showed me some interesting background information at work "behind the Bible" in this passage.

The Jews living during the time of Jesus knew the Temple and many of its most public functions. One of these better-known functions was the work of the Temple guards. Each night priests were assigned to posts to guard the Temple area. Throughout the night, the head of the Temple Guard with others carrying torches would walk from post to post to check on the priests standing watch. If he found a guard standing at his post, he would say to him "Peace to you." But if he found a guard sleeping at his post, the head of the Temple Guard would strike him with his stick. If worse punishment was needed, the guard's clothes would be torn off and burned, making him run home naked and ashamed.

When this background information is applied to Mark 14, some surprising details come to light. First, when Christ came to Gethsemane to pray with His disciples, and especially Peter, James, and John, they fell asleep. And what did Jesus say to them when he found them asleep? "Could you not keep watch for one hour?" (Mark 14:27)

Keep watch? What were they supposed to keep watch over? A possible answer is that they, like the Temple guards, were supposed to keep watch over Jesus, the true Temple (John 2:19-22).

When Judas and the priests, scribes, and elders came, the disciples "...all left him and fled" (Mark 14:50), but one disciple did not leave unpunished. Like the Temple guard who was caught asleep at his post, he was stripped of his clothing and ran off naked.

Another allusion to this practice appears in Revelation 16:15, where it says: "('Behold, I am coming like a thief.' Blessed is the one who watches and keeps his clothes ready, so that he may not go naked and people see him exposed.)"

In this passage, Jesus' Second Coming is likened to a thief who comes when the home owner least expects a break-in (cf. Matthew 24:42–44; 1 Thessalonians 5:2, Revelation 3:3). But the reference to clothing and the shame of being exposed doesn't make sense, unless perhaps it is harkening back to the Temple guard who sleeps at his post.

As you can see, this seemingly incidental detail in Mark may indeed be more significant than it first appears. We, too, need to keep watch and be vigilant. Otherwise, we may be put to shame at Christ's coming (1 John 2:28).

Mark 14:62 - What's Behind the High Priest's "Overreaction?"

One of the few things I remember from my college psychology classes is that sometimes an overreaction to an ordinary situation may be a signal that something more is going on than meet the eye. This is common sense. If an adult runs screaming at the first sight of a bee, chances are the overreaction stems from a bad experience with a bee. Scripture has its share of what seems like overreactions, but really they are signals for us to dig deeper behind the Bible.

One "overreaction" that puzzled me was that of the high priest during Jesus' trail. The high priest asked Our Lord, "Are you the Messiah?" And Jesus answered:

"I am; and 'you will see the Son of Man seated at the right hand of the Power and coming with the clouds of heaven.'"

You'd think that the high priest would be pleased to get an answer. But instead, the high priest tears his robes (which is forbidden in Leviticus 10:6 and 21:10) and says, "… 'What further need have we of witnesses? You have heard the blasphemy. What do you think?'…" (Mark 14:63-64).

Why such a violent reaction to Jesus' words? Clearly, there is more going on here than meets the eye.

One possible reason for the charge of blaspheme may be that when Jesus said "I am," he wasn't just saying "yes." The words "I am" happen to be the same words in the Greek Old Testament for God's name. When Moses asked God for His name, God replied, "I am who am" (Exodus 3:14). Since speaking the Divine Name in ancient Judaism was sacrilegious and worthy of capital punishment, Jesus' reply could explain the high priest's reaction. However, it is not at all clear that Jesus said the Divine Name. He may have just said, "I am [the Messiah]." If this is so, why did the high priest react like he did?

A better explanation that scholars (even Jewish scholars) have highlighted may be what Jesus says afterwards: "…you will see the Son of Man seated at the right hand of the Power and coming with the clouds of heaven."

These words come from the Book of Daniel. In Daniel 7:13-14, Daniel sees in a dream a vision of "One like a son of man coming, on the clouds of heaven; When he reached the Ancient One and was presented before him, He received dominion, glory, and kingship; nations and peoples of every language serve him. His dominion is an everlasting dominion that shall not be taken away, his kingship shall not be destroyed."

What may have caused the charge of blaspheme isn't so much Our Lord's application of this verse to Himself, since it certainly points to the Messiah but that He, the son of man, will be "…seated at the right hand of the Power" (Mark 14:62).

Just before Daniel 7:13-14, Daniel had another vision.

> "As I watched, Thrones were set up and the Ancient One took his throne … His throne was flames of fire, with wheels of burning fire. A surging stream of fire flowed out from where he sat; Thousands upon thousands were ministering to him, and myriads upon myriads attended him…" (Daniel 7:9-10).

What's interesting here is that Daniel saw more than one throne set up. The Ancient One, who is God, took one throne, but there is no mention of who takes the other throne. Some Jews have speculated that the Son of Man, when he received universal dominion over the earth, would take the other throne. Sounds reasonable, but if this is so, the Son of Man would be divine and enjoy divine prerogatives. When Jesus said he will come "seated at the right hand of the Power" and coming "on the clouds," he essentially put these two ideas together and claimed that he is the Messiah, the Son of Man, and God. The high priest also knew the implications of Jesus' words, and he ripped his robes in protest of the perceived blasphemy.

The next time you run across something in Scripture that seems to be an overreaction, watch out! There may be more going on behind the Bible.

The Gospel According to Luke

Just What the Doctor Ordered: St. Luke the Physician (Sept. 19, 2014)

All Scripture is inspired by God — meaning that the Holy Spirit is the primary author of Scripture. Inspiration, however, does not turn the human secondary authors into robots. Far from it. As the Second Vatican Council taught, the Holy Spirit "…made use of their [that is the human authors] powers and abilities, so that with Him acting in them and through them, they, as true authors, consigned to writing everything and only those things which He wanted" (Vatican II, Dogmatic Constitution on Divine Revelation, 3, 11). For this reason, each book uniquely reflects the style and experience of its author. The Gospel of Luke, for example, is a great example of how the Holy Spirit used Luke's knowledge and personality to uniquely shape his Gospel and the Acts of the Apostles.

You probably already know that St. Luke was a physician. St. Paul calls him "the beloved physician" in Colossians 4:14. One of the many fascinating things about St. Luke is how his occupation as a physician shaped and contributed to his writings.

For example, St. Luke begins his Gospel by stating his intention not to simply pass on what he had heard, but, like a good man of science, to investigate "everything accurately anew" and to "write it down in an orderly sequence" (Luke 1:3). His claim is backed up by his text, which draws upon several different sources, including details that could only have been known to eyewitness such as the events surrounding Christ's infancy.

How Bad is it, Doc?

Luke's sensitivities as a doctor also shows up in many subtle, and not so subtle, ways as when he recounts Christ's healing of Simon's mother-in-law. Mark, a non-physician, mentions the mother-in-law's fever but does not mention how bad of a fever it was (Mark 1:30). Luke, however, tells us that the fever was severe (Luke 4:38).

A similar attention to medical detail can be seen by comparing how Mark and Luke describe the condition of a leper in Mark 1:40 and Luke 5:12. Mark simply identifies him as a leper, while Luke notes that the man was "full of leprosy." Leprosy is a very contagious disease that can spread throughout the body. Luke takes care to note that this man's leprosy was in a very advanced stage.

A somewhat humorous and revealing contrast can also be found in how Mark and Luke describe the medical history of the woman afflicted with hemorrhages in Mark 5:25-27 and Luke 8:34-44. Mark describes:

"There was a woman afflicted with hemorrhages for twelve years. She had suffered greatly at the hands of many doctors and had spent all that she had. Yet she was not helped but only grew worse. She had heard about Jesus and came up behind him in the crowd and touched his cloak" (Mk 5:25-27).

Luke states the same facts of the case, albeit with a difference:

"And a woman afflicted with hemorrhages for twelve years, who (had spent her whole livelihood on doctors and) was unable to be cured by anyone, came up behind him and touched the tassel on his cloak. Immediately her bleeding stopped" (Luke 8:43-44).

Although St. Luke admitted that she had spent her whole livelihood on doctors, he neglected to mention that she had "suffered greatly" at their hands and that her condition "was not helped, but only grew worse." Apparently, Luke wished not to speak ill of his fellow practitioners.

Numerous other examples can be given as well, not only from Luke's Gospel, but also from the Acts of the Apostles, to show how the Holy Spirit was able to use Luke's training as a physician to make unique contributions to the New Testament.

The Holy Spirit worked in a special way in Luke. But the Holy Spirit also calls us to share and explain our faith. We all come from different backgrounds, levels of education, skills, and experiences that have molded and shaped our lives. How can we offer these things to the Holy Spirit to be used to make Christ better known and loved?

Luke 1:28 - Is Mary Full of Grace, or Just Highly Favored? (May 30, 2014)

From childhood we've prayed the Hail Mary with the words, "Hail Mary, full of grace…" These words come from the angel Gabriel's greeting to the Blessed Virgin in Luke 1:28. If you've looked up this verse in different Bibles, however, you may have noticed varying translations. What accounts for this, and what did the angel really said to Mary? To answer this, we need to dig into the background of Luke 1:28.

At the end of the fourth century, Pope St. Damasus commissioned St. Jerome to make a fresh Latin translation of the Bible. When St. Jerome came upon Luke 1:28, he translated the angel's title for Mary, the Greek word *kecharitomene,* into the Latin *"gratia plena"* ("full of grace"). Centuries later, Jerome's became the official translation of the Catholic Church, and English translations, such the Douay-Rheims Bible and the Knox, rendered it as "full of grace."

More recent Catholic translations render *kecharitomene* differently. Some say "favored one" (NAB) or "you who enjoy God's favor" (NJB). Protestant translations are even more varied. (For example, the King James Version reads, "O highly favored one," while the more interpretive God's Word Translation gives "you are favored by the Lord.") What accounts for these differences, and why are they important?

Getting to the Greek

The Greek language can pack a lot into a single word, which makes it difficult to convey all the nuances in English, so let's take a closer look at *kecharitomene* and see what it tells us.

The word is comprised of three parts: a root, a suffix, and a prefix. Each tells us something important.

The root of *kecharitomene* is *charitoo,* which is commonly translated "grace," a supernatural endowment gratuitously given by God (CCC 1997-1998). Scripture sometimes emphasizes what God gives — a supernatural gift (Luke 2:40, Acts 6:8) — and sometimes why God gives it — His favor or kindness (Acts 13:43, Gal. 1:15). Both are always present, because God's gift of divine help comes from his beneficence and God's beneficence is manifested by his divine help — which accounts for the different translations of "grace" or "favor."

The suffix *–mene* indicates a passive participle, meaning Mary (the subject) is being *acted upon*. This is important because it shows Mary *did not* bring herself into this graced state, but rather it was the action of God — it describes Mary as "she who has been graced [by God]."

The prefix *ke–* indicates the perfect tense — meaning the action (Mary's being graced) has been completed in the past with its results continuing in full effect.

What does it mean?

Gabriel's greeting, *kecharitomene,* means God's grace (favor) has been given to Mary prior to the angel's appearance and that graced state continues on. It hints at, but does not alone demonstrate, both Mary's Immaculate Conception — that Mary "…at the first instant of her conception…was preserved immaculate from all stain of original sin…" (Pope Pius IX, "Ineffabilis Deus") — and her subsequent sinless life of grace.

But what about St. Jerome's "full of grace"? Does *kecharitomene* have a sense of fullness? Yes, it does. The prefect tense carries with it a sense of fullness or completion. Take for example the word translated "it is written" (gegraptai). It too is in the perfect tense, and carries a sense of "It has been written and it stands written." It lacks nothing. Likewise, Mary has been graced (favored) by God and she stands in that grace (favor). She is full of grace.

This raises a problem for those who translate *kecharitomene* as "favor." How can the fullness or completeness of the perfect be expressed in terms of favor? Some try to intensify the word by giving "you who are highly favored" (NIV, NKJV, ISV, ASV) or "greatly blessed" (GNB) or "richly blessed" (NASB95, gloss).

The background to Gabriel's greeting tells us quite a bit about the "great things" God has done for Mary (Luke 1:49). It also explains why one Greek word has spawned so many different translations.

Luke 1:39-43, 56 - Seeing Mary as the Ark of the Covenant (Dec. 26, 2014)

Our approach to Scripture is very different than how the New Testament uses it. When we study Scripture, we usually start by picking a text and thinking about how it can be applied in our lives. When Christ came, however, the New Testament writers reversed the process. They experienced and observed Christ's life and looked to Scripture to better understand its significance.

A good example of this deep, meaningful exposition of the advent of Christ can be found in how St. Luke describes Mary's visitation to Elizabeth — in terms of the Ark of the Covenant returning to Jerusalem.

What is the Ark of the Covenant? Many confuse it with Noah's ark; the Ark of the Covenant, however, was the most sacred object in all of Israel. A gold-covered wooden chest, it contained the tablets of the Ten Commandments (Ex 25:16), a pot of manna from the Exodus (Ex 16:33), and Aaron's rod that blossomed

(Numbers 17:10; Heb 9:4). It also was the place where God's presence once overshadowed (Numbers 7:89).

In the account of the visitation of Mary with Elizabeth, Luke's account parallels the Old Testament story of David bringing the Ark of the Covenant to Jerusalem.

In 2 Samuel 6, Scripture records how King David brought the Ark of the Covenant to Jerusalem. David and all the people arose and went to Baal-Judah with great celebration (2 Samuel 6:1-2). But there was a big problem: They didn't carry the Ark as God had commanded. They brought it on a cart, when God said it should be carried using poles by the Levites to prevent anyone from touching this most sacred object (Ex 25:13-14; Deut. 31:9, Josh. 3:3). Along the way, the oxen stumbled, and Uzzah, one of the attendants, placed his hand on the Ark to steady it and was immediately struck dead (2 Sam. 6:6-8).

Dave became afraid and exclaimed, "How can the ark of the LORD come to me?" (2 Samuel 6:9) and they left the Ark at the house of Obed-edom the Gittite for three months (2 Samuel 6:11). When David heard that God had blessed Obed-edom's household, he decided to bring the Ark of the Covenant into Jerusalem the right way and with even greater pomp, offering sacrifices every six steps. Moreover, David, dressed in a priestly garment, danced with abandon before the Ark (2 Samuel 6:14). The Ark was greeted with shouts of joy and trumpet blasts (2 Sam. 6:15), and David blessed the people (2 Sam. 6:19).

Why is all this important? St. Luke, learning about Mary's visitation to Elizabeth, looks to 2 Samuel 6 to see its significance.

Compare Luke 1:39-43, 56 with 2 Samuel 6, and you'll see several very interesting parallels:

- Both David and Mary "arose" and made the journey to Judah (2 Sam. 6:2, Luke 1:39)

- Both David (dressed like a priest) and John the Baptist (the son of a priest) in Elizabeth's womb "danced" or "leaped" (2 Sam. 6:14, Luke 1:43). The same Greek word is used in both texts.

- David and the people shout for joy before the Ark just as Elizabeth shouts for joy before Mary (2 Sam. 6:15, Luke 1:42).

- David asked, "How can the ark of the Lord come to me?" (2 Samuel 6:9) while Elizabeth asks, "And how has it happened to me, that the mother of my Lord would come to me?" (Luke 1:43).

- The Ark remained at Obed-edom's house for three months (2 Samuel 6:11). Mary remained at Elizabeth's house for three months (Luke 1:56).

These parallels are not by accident. St. Luke is taking a historical event and looking to Scripture (i.e., the Old Testament) to better understand its significance. By doing so, he sees Mary as the "ark" of the New Covenant. How so? Just as God's presence once overshadowed the Ark, the Holy Spirit overshadowed Mary when she conceived Jesus (Luke 1:35).

The Ark also contained within it the Ten Commandments, the manna (bread from heaven), and Aaron's rod. Mary's womb contained Christ, the fulfillment of all three of these signs: the

Word of God (the commandments), the true bread from heaven, and high priest (signified by Aaron's rod). In a very real way, Mary becomes for the New Testament what the Ark of the Covenant was to the Old Testament: God's chosen vessel.

Luke 1:48 - Mary, Jerusalem, and the Problem of Praise (June 12, 2015)

"How can you focus on Christ when you Catholics honor Mary so much?" It might be surprising to Catholics that devotions such as our Litany of Loreto, in which we extol Mary with honorific titles (all of them rooted in Christ, by the way), appear to non-Catholics as strange and unbiblical.

The funny thing is, the Bible doesn't really support such an opinion. Scripture doesn't pit praising God to the exclusion of extolling his mighty works in creation. On the contrary, Scripture sees recognizing, praising and extolling God's works in creation as just another way to honor and glorify God.

Case in point is how the Old Testament speaks of the city of Jerusalem. Even though Jerusalem is just another man-made city, Scripture praises it in many extravagant ways. It is called "the city of God" (Psalms 46:4; 48:1), "the city of the Lord" (Isaiah 60:14), "the city of the great king" (Psalms 48:2; Matthew 5:35), "city of righteousness" (Isaiah 1:26), "the city of truth" (Zechariah 8:3), "holy city" (Nehemiah 11:1, Isaiah 48:2, Matthew 4:5), "the throne of the Lord" (Jeremiah 3:17), "Zion of the holy one of Israel" (Isaiah 60:14), "the all-beautiful city," and "the joy of the whole earth" (Psalms 48:1-3, Lamentations 2:15). Jerusalem is said to be "highly praised" (Psalms 48:1), and the abode of Justice and the holy hill (Jeremiah 31:23). Psalms 137:6 goes so far as to say, "May my tongue cling to the roof of my mouth if I do not remember you, if I do not exalt Jerusalem above my chief joy."

How can Scripture give such incredible praise to a mere created thing? Jerusalem is praised and placed "above my chief joy" because God has done great things for Jerusalem. He dwelt within it.

Mary is a lot like Jerusalem in this respect. In fact, if you read closely Luke's account of the Annunciation, you'll find Mary is described in a way similar to how God addressed "Zion" (i.e., Jerusalem) in Zephaniah 3:14-18.

For example, at the Annunciation, the angel Gabriel addresses Mary, not with the customary "Peace" (Shalom), but with "Rejoice!" This mirrors the same way God address Jerusalem in Zephaniah, "Shout for joy, O daughter Zion! Sing joyfully, O Israel! Be glad and exult with all your heart, O daughter Jerusalem!" (Zephaniah 3:14).

The reason Zion is to rejoice is because "the Lord is in your midst" (Zephaniah 3:15), much like Gabriel's words to Mary, "…the Lord is with you" (Luke 1:28).

Furthermore, Mary was troubled and pondered what sort of greeting this was. The angel then tells her, "Don't be afraid…" (Luke 1:30). Likewise, Zephaniah 3:16 says, "On that day, it shall be said to Jerusalem: Fear not, O Zion, be not discouraged!"

The last contact with Zephaniah is difficult to see in English. Zephaniah says to Jerusalem, "The LORD, your God, is in your midst, a mighty savior." Literally, "Yahweh, a mighty savior, is in your midst." The Hebrew word translated "in your midst" can also be translated "in your womb" depending on whether it applies to a person or an objection. Since Zephaniah is speaking about

Jerusalem, translators render the word "in your midst." But if this passage is applied to Mary, it would mean "in your womb."

Here is where things get interesting: Gabriel tells Mary, "Behold, you will conceive in your womb and bear a son, and you shall name him Jesus" (Luke 1:31). Mary is going to conceive Jesus in her womb. Now, the name Jesus in Hebrew is *Yeshua*. It is a compound of two words: "Yahweh," the divine name of God, and "Savoir." It means "Yahweh-Savoir" or "Yahweh Saves." In other

words, Mary will have "Yah[weh]-Savior" in her womb just like Zephaniah's word to Jerusalem that Yahweh, a mighty savoir, is in Jerusalem's midst.

Gabriel speaks to Mary as Zephaniah spoke to Jerusalem. Therefore, if the Old Testament can highly praise and exalt Jerusalem because God dwelt within it, it is perfectly in-line with Scripture for Catholics to praise, exalt, and magnify Mary because God has done great things for her (Luke 1:49), and raise her above our "chief joy."

Luke 1:71-74 - Total Recall: Early Christian Memory Devices in the Benedictus (July 10, 2014)

"Every Good Boy Does Fine," my music teacher said, pointing to the staff lines of the music sheet. "The notes are E-G-B-D-F." Over the years, I still remember the exact note order of the lines on the treble clef because of that little mnemonic device. Mnemonic devices such as this have helped untold millions recall complex data quickly and accurately.

They also played a very important role for cultures, such as ancient Judaism, which relied on oral tradition to pass on information. Rabbis would present lessons in formats conducive to memorization. By structuring lessons in helpful ways (i.e., literary forms), using word play and other techniques, the rabbis helped their disciples memorize and accurately recall hundreds of lines of Scripture and legislation.

Solving the Puzzle

One passage of Scripture you may have read and prayed a hundred times — The Prayer of Zechariah or the *Benedictus* (Luke 1:68-75) — but did you know there's a memory device being used in the text?

Before we begin, however, a word about the Gospels: The oldest copies of the New Testament were written in Greek. Scholars have long noticed the Greek in the Gospels does not always read like Greek. Sometimes the text sounds like a Hebrew or Aramaic person speaking in the Greek tongue. In other words, it appears portions of the Greek Gospels are translations of an early Semitic source, either Hebrew or Aramaic. This is not a new idea. The French scholar Jean Carmignac in his book *The Birth of the Synoptics* chronicles dozens of works over the last few centuries that have recognized an underlying Semitic text and even attempted to back-translate the Greek into Hebrew or Aramaic.

On the surface, this may sound easy. But it's not. It's easy to translate one language into another, but it is not always possible to look at a translation and know its original wording. For example, we find the Greek word "agape" and we translate it as "love." A few years pass and we lose our original text. We see the word "love," but what was the original text? The Greek language has four words that could be translated "love" *(agape, eros, philia, and storge)*. How would we know which is the correct word? Although the context may help narrow our choices, ultimately our back-translation is a little more than an educated guess.

The Prayer of Zechariah

However, there are instances where special features in a text (such as a word play) can reveal the original text. One such instance is a section in the *Benedictus* (Luke 1:71-74), which reads:

71 ....salvation from our enemies and from the hand of all who hate us,

72 to show mercy to our fathers and to be mindful of his holy covenant

73 and of the oath he swore to Abraham our father, and to grant us that,

74 rescued from the hand of enemies, without fear we might worship him.

Carmignac points out that the Hebrew translation of verses 72-73 appears to make a three-fold allusion to the names John (the Baptist), Zechariah, and Elizabeth. To see this, we must look at these names in Hebrew.

In Hebrew, John is *Yohanan*. It's root *hanan* means "to show mercy."

Zechariah in Hebrew is *Zakaryah*. It's root *zakar* means "to remember."

Elizabeth is *Elishaba*. It's Hebrew root *shaba* means "to swear an oath."

This cluster of allusions to John, Zechariah, and Elizabeth could not be coincidental; rather, it appears to be a memory device embedded in Luke's original Semitic source. We can also add that this three-fold allusion is sandwiched between two lines that refer to the "hands" of enemies (Luke 1:71, 74). Could it be that the reference to hands would flag the disciple memorizing to follow with the allusions to John, Zechariah, and Elizabeth to ensure that the lines "to show mercy…" "to remember…" and "the oath that is sworn…" would be recited correctly?

This, and dozens of other instances like it, shows that Christians from the beginning did not pass on the faith on as a fluid mishmash of unrelated information, but like the rabbis of their age they took great care to ensure what they handed on would be accurately and authentically transmitted to future generations.

Luke 11:50 (Matthew 23:35) - Did Jesus Give Us Bible Bookends?

Did Jesus ever tell us which books belong in the Old Testament? Many Protestants argue that he did and they appeal to Jesus' words concerning the shedding of the prophets blood being "from the blood of Abel to the blood of Zechariah, the son of Berechiah ..." (Luke 11:50, Mathew 23:35). It is argued that according to the traditional order of Old Testament books, Jesus is using examples taken from the first book (i.e., Abel in Genesis) and the last book (i.e., Zechariah in Second Chronicles). Because this is the same book order as the rabbinical Bible, it is argued, Jesus must have accepted the rabbinical canon (which omits the seven deuterocanonical books Catholics and Orthodox accept). Is this a sound argument? Not at all.

Although the argument firmly states that Jesus is referring to Zechariah, the son of Jehoiada (2 Chronicles 24:20-22), the question has puzzled scholars for centuries, as no one seems to exactly fit our Lord's description. Zechariah of Chronicles doesn't fit because Jesus identifies Zechariah as "the son of Berechiah" (Matthew 23:35), not "the son of Jehoiada. Jesus also says to his hearers, concerning Zechariah, "...whom you murdered between the sanctuary and the altar." But the son of Jehoiada was murdered centuries earlier.

Another candidate is the prophet Zechariah, who is twice called "the son of Berechiah" (Zechariah 1:1, 7). However, Scripture is silent as to how the prophet died and he too (like the son of Jehoiada) was not a contemporary of Jesus. Zechariah, John the Baptist's father, is also a candidate. In a previous article, we saw that there was an early Christian tradition that he was martyred in the temple area. The only problem is Scripture does not tell us Zechariah's father, nor does it tell us how he died.

It's also possible that Jesus was referring to an otherwise unknown Zechariah who had recently been murdered. After all, this would be no different than the other times Jesus mentions contemporary events that are not otherwise recorded in Scripture, such as the 18 people being killed by the falling tower of Siloam (Luke 13:4). Maybe Jesus is doing the same thing here? In any case, identifying Jesus' Zechariah is not as easy as it seems. But even if Jesus did refer to the Zechariah in Second Chronicles, was Chronicles always the last book in the Jewish Bible?

This point is even more speculative than the first. There is only one Jewish list in all of antiquity that places Chronicles at the end of the Hebrew Bible (*b. Baba Bathra*, 14b). Every early Church fathers, who attempted to reproduce the contents of the Jewish Bible, ended his list with either Esther or Ezra-Nehemiah. None of them put Chronicles last. Even the oldest complete Hebrew Bibles (the Aleppo and Leningrad codices) place Chronicles first among the Writings, not last. The earliest evidence of any Jewish writing putting Chronicles last, outside of *b. Baba Bathra* 14b, is from the 13th century!

You're probably asking yourself, if this is true, how can this order be said to be the "traditional order" when there doesn't seem to be any tradition supporting it? The answer is the printing press. When Hebrew Bibles began to be printed, the book publishers placed Chronicles last. Soon, every major printed copy of the Hebrew text from the 15th century onward ended with Chronicles. It's "traditional," not because it was an ancient common practice, but because it was the traditional way book publishers printed Hebrew Bibles.

As you can see, the "bookends" argument doesn't have a leg to stand on. But even if we grant all the argument's premises, it still doesn't follow that Jesus meant for Abel and Zechariah to refer to the first and last books of Bible. There are other perfectly good reasons for why Jesus picked these two examples. It is quite likely that they were chosen simply because they were examples of two deaths that demanded retribution (Genesis 4:10, 2 Chronicles 24:22). If this is so, it doesn't matter which books recorded their deaths and Jesus' words would have no bearing on the order of books.

The Gospel According to John

John 1:1 - The Genesis of John's Prologue: The Background Behind "the Word"

Even those who don't read the Bible frequently are familiar with the prologue to St. John's Gospel, since it's among the most quoted and memorized words of the New Testament:

"In the beginning was the Word, and the Word was with God, and the Word was God. He was in the beginning with God. All things came to be through him, and without him nothing came to be. What came to be through him was life, and this life was the light of the human race; the light shines in the darkness, and the darkness has not overcome it" (John 1:1-4).

This passage can be so familiar to us that we may forget to ask a very basic and important question: Where did John find the image of God's Word for our pre-incarnate Lord, and what does it mean?

We know that the idea of "the word" (Greek, *logos*) played a significant role in Greek philosophy. For them, the *logos* was a divine utterance, a manifestation of a god, or even an emanation coming forth from a god. However, John's source was not Greek philosophy, but the Old Testament, which had a very developed and deep understanding of God's Word.

It is no accident that John begins his Gospel with the exact same words that begin the book of Genesis. John 1:1 and Genesis 1:1 both begin with the words, "In the beginning…" John's prologue also contains elements found in the first chapter of Genesis, such as light, darkness, and life.

Of course, the most important connection between these two passages is God's Word. Yet, if you compare John with Genesis 1, you'll see that John seems to go beyond what is said of the Word in Genesis.

In Genesis, the Word seems impersonal and veiled. Unlike John, it isn't singled out in the narrative being reference indirectly as "God said." But as the Scripture unfolds, more light is revealed about God's Word. For example, in Psalm 33:6, God's Word is singled out and it becomes the focus of God's creative action: "By the LORD'S word the heavens were made; by the breath of his mouth all their host." In Isaiah 55:11, God's Word is sent as an agent to accomplish His will before returning back to Him.

By the time we get to the last Old Testament books to be written, God's Word is described, not as an impersonal utterance as in Genesis 1, but as God's Wisdom personified as in Sirach 24:3, where Sirach speaks in the person of the Word saying, "From the mouth of the Most High I came forth, and mistlike covered the earth. In the highest heavens did I dwell, my throne on a pillar of cloud." Notice how Sirach echoes Genesis 1, but that the Word is not an impersonal utterance, but personified Wisdom that is distinct from the Most High, yet enthroned with the Most High in heaven.

The Book of Wisdom likewise sees God's Word is nothing other than His Wisdom (cf. Wisdom 9:1-2, 1 Corinthians 1:24). In Wisdom 7:23-24, God's Wisdom is described using terms that are exclusive to God alone. Wisdom is called "all-powerful," "unique" (or "only-begotten"), "all-seeing," and "pervading all things." In other words, God's Wisdom / Word is wholly unique, omnipotent, omniscient, and omnipresent, attributes possessed by God alone.

This brings us right up to the doorstep of the New Testament era. Non-biblical Jewish writings composed around the time of Christ likewise brings out the mystery that God's Word is both God and yet in some way not the same as the Creator. The Targums (Aramaic translations of the Scripture) depict God's Word (Aramaic, *memra*) as living, active, and speaking, sometimes even using it as a substitute for the divine name. Philo of Alexandria seems to have understood the Word to be a kind of divine mediator between the infinite God and humanity.

By the time of Christ, the theological ground had already been prepared for His arrival. Christ unlocks this mystery: He is the Word, the Second Person of the Trinity, who was with God and is God. John's prologue beautifully connects all these dots.

John 1:45-50 - In Nathaniel's Calling, There's More Than Meets the Eye (January 13, 2017)

The calling of the apostles is pretty much straightforward. Jesus walks up to fishermen and calls them to follow him and to become "fishers of men." The meaning is deep, but not very mysterious. The same cannot be said for the calling of Nathaniel. Unlike the usual, "Come follow me," Nathaniel and Jesus enter into a short dialogue that seems on the surface to be very odd.

The narrative begins with Philip telling Nathaniel that he had found the one prophesied by Moses and the prophets, Jesus of Nazareth. Nathaniel was not impressed and says to Philip, "Can anything good come from Nazareth?" Philip invites Nathaniel to "come and see." While still a ways off, Jesus sees Nathaniel and says to him, "Here is a true Israelite. There is no duplicity in him." Nathaniel's answer is sometimes translated poorly. Nathaniel doesn't reply, "How do you know me?" like we'd expect him to say. Instead, he says, "Where do you know me?" Jesus answered, "Before Philip called you, I saw you under the fig tree." Nathaniel responds, "Rabbi, you are the Son of God; you are the King of Israel" (John 1:45-50).

If you're like me, you probably have the feeling that there is more going on in this passage than meets the eye. For example, why did Nathaniel have a problem with Nazareth? Why did he ask Jesus, "Where do you know me?" instead of, "How do you know me?" And why would Nathaniel assume Jesus is the Messiah King simply because he saw him under a fig tree? Certainly, Nathaniel recognized something that we don't. But what?

Let's begin by noting that it all begins with Philip and Nathaniel's discussion about Nazareth. Philip identifies the Messiah as "Jesus of Nazareth," and Nathaniel asks, "Can anything good come out of Nazareth?" Why focus on Nazareth?

Nazareth is a Hebrew name that has for its root the word "netzer," which means "branch" or "shoot." The figure of a "branch" or "shoot" is commonly associated with the Messiah King (Isaiah 11:1, Jeremiah 23:5, etc.). As we will see, this will be important.

Next, Nathaniel accepts Philip's invitation and leaves his fig tree to go see this person from the town of "shoot" or "branch." When Jesus sees Nathaniel coming to him, he calls him "a true Israelite." Nathaniel responses, "Where do you know me?" On one level, this is the first time Nathaniel meets Jesus, so it is a logical question. It's also possible that Nathaniel knew of the messianic prophecy in Zechariah 3:8, 10, which says:

> "Listen, O Joshua, high priest! You and your associates who sit before you are men of good omen. Yes, I will bring my servant the Shoot … On that day, says the LORD of hosts, you will invite one another under your vines and fig trees." (Zechariah 3:8, 11).

Notice that Zechariah calls the Messiah, "the Shoot," and says that in the days of the Messiah the Israelites will "invite one another under your vines and fig trees" just like Philip invited Nathaniel. Nathaniel, being a true Israelite, accepted the invitation and came out. Perhaps wondering if this was a mere coincidence, he asked Jesus "where" he knew him. Jesus answered, "Before Philip called you, I saw you under the fig tree." It was no coincidence that Nathaniel, a true Israelite, was invited to meet Jesus of Nazareth (the Shoot) from under a fig tree. This is exactly what Zechariah foresaw. Realizing this, Nathaniel proclaims, "Rabbi, you are the Son of God; you are the King of Israel." Jesus answered, "Do you believe because I told you that I saw you under the fig tree? You will see greater things than this." Indeed, not only would Nathaniel see the fulfillment of Zechariah 3:8, 11, but ultimately the fulfillment of all that was written about the Messiah by Moses and the prophets.

John 2:6 - What was so Funny at the Wedding at Cana? (Feb. 20, 2015)

The Gospel of John wonderfully depicts Our Lord's life in a way that is accessible to both the average person as well as the scholar. The wedding at Cana is a great example of how John's narrative is both easy to understand and enjoyable to the reader yet at the same time deep and profound. In fact, there is an element of humor at the wedding at Cana that unless you look a little deeper "Behind the Bible," you may have missed.

Our familiarity with this miracle sometimes works against us in that we gloss over the details of the story because they are so familiar to us. But let's take ourselves off autopilot and look at the details with fresh eyes. Christ turned water to wine. Did you ever notice where the servant got the water for the miracle? St. John tells us:

> "Now there were six stone water jars there for Jewish ceremonial washings, each holding twenty to thirty gallons" (John 2:6).

What were these stone water jars, and why were they at the wedding? They we used for ritual washing. Washing rituals were very important to the people of the Old Testament. The Pharisees once complained that Christ's disciples were eating with unwashed hands. They took offense, not because they were afraid of spreading germs, but because they interpreted Leviticus 15:11 in a very strict sense (Matthew 15:2). By ritually washing your hands before a meal, you cleansed yourself from any ritual defilement you might have previously contracted. It's also interesting that John mentions these jars were made of stone, not earthenware. This fits perfectly with rabbinical teaching that unlike earthenware, stone could not be ritually defiled.

We should also note the size of these six stone jars. When we think of the miracle at Cana, we often picture a few containers of water being turned into wine. But John tells us that each jar contained approximately 20 to 30 gallons! That means Jesus' miracle produced more wine than could possibility be needed for the feast.

The number of jars is also interesting because the number six often represents imperfection or incompleteness and perhaps points to the Old Covenant. Case in point: In the Old Covenant, we are to work six days and rest on the Sabbath (the seventh).

You can begin to see both the depth of Christ's miracle and also an element of humor. Christ took the water used for ritual cleansing in the Old Covenant and transformed it into the best wine of the wedding feast. This episode is so deep that we will have to save these elements for future articles, but for now I'd like to focus on the humorous element.

Jesus didn't transform drinking water into wine. The water supplied for this miracle was anything but clean. It was hand-washing water! It definitely would not be the type of water anyone would voluntarily drink. The funny part? Christ commanded the waiters to give it to the headwaiter, their boss.

When he tasted it, he proclaimed it was the best wine of the feast. Why did the headwaiter drink the hand-washing water? John tells us the headwaiter did not know where it came from (although the servers who had drawn the water knew) (John 2:9). I imagine the waiters grinning as they handed the water to their boss. Still, you have to admire the faith of the wait staff. Can you imagine serving your boss the same thing?

I think this humorous element gives us something to ponder during Lent. Heaven is our goal and Mass is a foretaste of the Wedding Supper of the Lamb that we will enjoy with Christ at the end of time. But first we need to be prepared for the feast. We need to be like the obedient waiters at Cana who followed Mary's command, "Do whatever he tells you" (John 2:5). We should do so with a smile because what may seem strange to the world will, in God's hands, bring about something unexpectedly wonderful.

John 4:4-30 - Finding a Bride at a Local Watering Hole (September 4, 2015)

When we write, our words symbolize or point to things. God, however, is so great that not only do His words symbolize, but even things symbolize or point to other things since He is the Lord of history and his Providence directs all.

I wish I could remember which early Church Father said this, because it is a profound explanation of why sacred history recounted in the Bible is more than a historical narrative; it is a meta-story. For this reason, the whole Bible (even the Old Testament) is relevant for us today — not so we know how to invade some future Canaanites, but that we can apply, by analogy, what is written to our own struggle against the world, the flesh, and the devil. As Paul says in 1 Corinthians 10:6, "These things happened as examples for us…"

Jesus is the Lord of history, and nothing in Christ's ministry happened by chance. Every place and event recorded in the Gospels is rich in meaning. We only have to discover what it is.

Take, for example, Jesus' conversation with the Samaritan woman at the well (John 4:4-30). Jesus was heading from Judea to Galilee. Most Jews took a long route around Samaria so as to avoid the Samaritans because Jews and Samaritans weren't exactly on friendly terms. But Jesus chooses to go through Samaria and meets a woman at a well. For most of us, this seems a bit routine. There's nothing significant about a man and a woman talking at a well, or is there?

Jesus meets the Samaritan woman at the well in this 19th century work from the Library of Congress. Because wells in biblical times were often meeting places for those looking to find a bride, Jesus' encounter suggests a deeper relationship between God, the heavenly bridegroom, and his wayward people in Samaria.

In biblical times, meeting at a well is something akin to going on an online dating service. Well, maybe not as crass or unseemly as that, but it was a place to find a bride. For example, Abraham placed his head servant under oath to go to his land and find a wife for his son Isaac. The servant went to the land and waited for evening outside the city of Nahor by the watering hole for the women of the city to come out to draw water. The servant prayed, "LORD, God of my master Abraham, let it turn out favorably for me today and thus deal graciously with my master Abraham. While I stand here at the spring and the daughters of the townsmen are coming out to draw water, if I say to a girl, 'Please lower your jug, that I may drink,' and she answers, 'Take a drink, and let me give water to your camels, too,' let her be the one whom you have decided upon for your servant Isaac. In this way I shall know that you have dealt graciously with my master" (Genesis 24:12-14). Immediately after he made this prayer, Rebecca came out.

The narrative continues, "...the servant ran toward her and said, 'Please give me a sip of water from your jug.' 'Take a drink, sir,' she replied, and quickly lowering the jug onto her hand, she gave him a drink. When she had let him drink his fill, she said, 'I will draw water for your camels, too, until they have drunk their fill.'" (Genesis 24:17-19). After she finished giving water, the servant knew Rebecca was the bride for Isaac. Likewise, Isaac's son Jacob also met his future wife Rachael at a well (Genesis 29:1-30). The same is true with Moses finding his wife Zipporah after visiting a well (Exodus 2:15-21). Wells are where women are called to be brides.

With this in mind, let's look at Jesus meeting the Samaritan woman at the well. Jesus says to her essentially the same thing Abraham's servant said to Rebecca, "Give me a drink" (John 4:7). As we will see in a future article, the dialogue between Jesus and the woman is more than a chat over a cool drink on a hot day; it's a dialogue between God (the Bridegroom) and Samaria (who has left her husband).

The significance of this conversion can be overlooked if you miss the biblical connection between wells and watering holes, brides and bridegrooms.

John 4:17-18 - Who were the Samaritan Woman's Five Husbands? (April 28, 2016)

When Jesus was traveling from Judea to Galilee, he took an unusual route. He went through Samaria. Samaritans and Jews were not on friendly terms and most Jews tried to avoid that route. Instead, our Lord made his way through Samaria, resting at a place called Jacob's well, where he asks a Samaritan woman for a drink.

We're all pretty familiar with this meeting in John 4, but have you ever noticed how their conversation takes a strange turn at the end?

Let's quickly outline the path of their conversation: Jesus asks for a drink. The Samaritan woman is surprised at his request because Jews use nothing in common with Samaritans. Jesus responds that if she knew who he was she'd ask him for "living water." When she said she would like this "living water," Jesus asks her to get her husband.

Stop. OK, that's the first odd turn in this conversation. What makes Jesus ask for her husband now after she expressed a desire to receive the "living water" that satisfies every thirst? The woman responds, "I don't have a husband" and Jesus replies, "You are right in saying, 'I do not have a husband.' For you have had five husbands, and the one you have now is not your husband" (John 4:17-18).

Her response takes another odd turn. First, she says, "Sir, I can see that you are a prophet." That makes sense. How else would Jesus know about her checkered past? But then she says something very odd: "…Our ancestors worshiped on this mountain; but you people say that the place to worship is in Jerusalem." Where did that come from? Why would the Samaritan woman suddenly change subjects from marriage to the nature of true worship? Why did this conversation make these strange twists and turns?

A little digging reveals one possible answer.

A feature of John's Gospels is that conversations often take place on two levels. For example, when Nicodemus visited Jesus at night, Jesus told him, "… no one can see the kingdom of heaven unless he is born from above" or "born again." Nicodemus misunderstands Jesus to be speaking about physical birth, when Jesus is actually talking about supernatural rebirth in baptism (John 3:1-12). The same might be true here.

On the earthly level, Jesus and the Samaritan woman are discussing her current matrimonial history, but there seems to be more going on here. The Samaritan's personal history seems to have run parallel to the religious history of Samaria.

Samaria was once part of the northern kingdom of Israel, which had broken off from the Davidic Kingdom. It had set up its own monarchy and form of worship until Assyria invaded and sent most of its inhabitants into exile. The king of Assyria brought pagans into Samaria to settle there (1 Kings 17:24).

Interestingly enough, 1 Kings 17:30-31 tells us there were five groups that settled there, each worshipping their own pagan gods: The Babylonians worshipped Marduk; the men of Cuth worshipped Nergal; the men of Avva worshipped Nibhaz and Tartak; the men of Sepharvaim worshipped their city gods; and King Hadad worshipped Anath.

Even though the Israelites were joined in covenant to the one true God, they intermarried with these foreigners and adopted their worship and practices. This is why the Jews wouldn't have anything in common with Samaritans — because their assimilation with these pagans had defiled them. Samaria, like the woman at the well, had five husbands and was estranged from her true husband.

If this is true, the transition from talking about "five husbands" to "true worship" naturally follows. Samaria's checkered past had distorted its worship, insisting that true worship must take place on Mount Gerizim, not in the temple in Jerusalem. Jesus' message to the woman and Samaria is that he fulfills all that the temple signified and will unite Samaritans, Jews, and all peoples together to worship God in spirit and truth.

John 7:37 - From Spring to King: How Jesus' "living water" Proclaimed His Identity (March 4, 2016)

It's amazing how often Jesus does or says something unexpected in the New Testament. These actions are usually surprising because we don't understand the surrounding historical context.

For example, did you ever wonder why, "On the last and greatest day of the feast, Jesus stood up and exclaimed, 'Let anyone who thirsts come to me and drink'" (John 7:37)?

What? Were the feast-goers thirsty? Why say such a thing at this point in time? And even more strange, why did the people after Jesus' words begin to ask whether he could be the Messiah (John

7:40-43)? What does the Messiah have to do with water? But the feast itself might provide us with some clues.

The feast being celebrated was the Feast of Tabernacles, also called the Feast of Booths (Hebrew, *Sukkot*). It's a major feast that is celebrated in harvest season when the grain is threshed and grapes are pressed. All three elements echo themes in Jesus' ministry. Jesus likened the gathering of converts to a harvest and the bread (grain) and wine point to the Eucharist. But where does the water come in?

Each day of the feast had a water ceremony. According to rabbinical sources, water was drawn from the Pool of Siloam and taken in procession to the water-gate of the Temple while a trumpet was blown amid shouts of joy. On the east side of the altar was a silver bowl for the water and the west had another for wine. Both bowls were poured out simultaneously on the altar.

OK, there's nothing about the Messiah here — that is, until you look into the historical background of this water.

The water in the Pool of Siloam did not originate there. It came via a tunnel constructed by King Hezekiah from a spring in Gihon. This spring is known as "The King's Pool" (Nehemiah 2:14) or "Solomon's Pool" (Josephus). The King's Pool? How did it get that name?

When King David decided that his son Solomon should become king after him, he did something strange. He didn't have Solomon anointed king in Jerusalem, but sent him out with a priest (Abiathar), a prophet (Nathan), and the king's official (Benaiah) to anoint him king in Gihon. Rabbinical tradition notes that "Kings are anointed only at the side of a spring, so that their rule may be prolonged" (b. Keritot, 1:1, v. 18b). Therefore, the son of David was anointed king next to "the King's Pool" in Gihon. Afterward, the king made a procession to Jerusalem amid trumpet blasts and joyful cries that followed him to take his throne (1 Kings 1:32-34). Solomon's anointing and enthronement sound awfully like the water used during the Feast of Tabernacles.

But the water ceremony of the Feast of Tabernacles wasn't a commemoration of Solomon's enthronement, but an anticipation of the long-awaited son of David, the Messiah King. Therefore, when Jesus says, "Let anyone who thirsts come to me and drink," he is essentially saying "I am what the water symbolized; I am the Messiah."

But there is more. Jesus also says, "Whoever believes in me, as Scripture says: 'Rivers of living water will flow from within him.'" (John 7:38). John notes that this refers to the Spirit that will be given to believers.

The giving of the Spirit is certainly symbolized by the pouring out of the water and wine on the altar, as Scripture often speaks about the Spirit being "poured out" (Proverbs 1:23, Isaiah 32:15, *et al.*). But what Scripture is Jesus quoting? Scholars are divided. There doesn't seem to be an exact match. One possibility might be Zechariah 14:8-9, which says "On that day, living waters shall flow from Jerusalem ... The LORD shall become king over the whole earth ..."

Notice how Zechariah links the flowing of living water with an enthronement. If this is so, then Jesus is saying much more than that he will provide refreshment for people. He's really suggesting that he is indeed the awaited Messiah King, who, at his enthronement, will pour out living water. It would explain why, after hearing Jesus, the people asked whether he could be the Messiah, the son of David.

John 8:1-11 - Getting Caught in Your Own Trap (June 12, 2014)

The first thing that comes to mind when reading the passage in the New Testament about the woman caught in adultery (John 8:1-11) is our Lord's profound example of justice and mercy. The background to this passage reveals that his example takes place within a potentially deadly game of entrapment.

When the scribes and Pharisees approached Jesus with the woman, they were not seeking his advice. The Law of Moses was quite clear on the point, as the scribes and Pharisees themselves point out (John 8:5). Leviticus 20:10 and Deuteronomy 22:22 make adultery a capital offense. Why, then, did they approach Jesus with this problem? John 8:6 tells us that they were "…testing Him, so that they might have grounds for accusing Him" (John 8:6). It is here that a little background reveals the nature of their trap.

During this time, Judea was ruled by the pagan Romans. Although the Romans conceded some measure of authority to the Sanhedrin, they did not give it the *ius gladii* or power of execution. Only Roman authorities could administer capital punishment. This is why the Jews handed Jesus over to the Romans to be executed by crucifixion (John 18:31).

The Roman usurpation of the power of execution made it impossible for the Jews to carry out various Mosaic prescriptions that called for capital punishment, such as the penalty for committing adultery in Leviticus 20:10 and Deuteronomy 22:22. If the Jews did execute someone or even incite others to do so, that action would itself be a capital offense against Roman law. Herein lies the trap.

Had Jesus said, "We must carry out the Law of Moses. Let her be stoned." The Pharisees would have grounds for accusing Jesus of inciting the people to break Roman law. But if Jesus put aside the Law of Moses because of political circumstances, he could hardly been seen as the Messiah. After all, what kind of Messiah would dismiss the Law of Moses for mere political expediency? Either choice would be disastrous.

What does Jesus do? He bends down and writes in the sand (John 8:6). Scripture does not record what Jesus wrote. Many have speculated as to what it could be. The fact that he wrote in the sand calls to mind Jeremiah 17:13, which reads, "O Lord, the hope of Israel: all that forsake thee shall be confounded: they that depart from thee, shall be written in the earth: because they have forsaken the Lord, the vein of living waters."

After pressing Jesus for an answer, Jesus responses, "Let the one among you who is without sin be the first to throw a stone at her." It is often thought that Christ is trying to prick the conscience of his hearers so they realize they are sinners just like the adulterous woman. But this could hardly be true for the Pharisees.

The Pharisees were the strictest sect in Judaism (Acts 26:5). Their name comes from the Hebrew *persahim* from the word *parash,* meaning "to separate." In other words, they were separated from ordinary sinners by their strict obedience to the Mosaic law. They believed that by keeping every precept of the Law, they would be justified before God. In this regard, they saw themselves as perfect, as St. Paul says about his former way of life as a Pharisee, "…in righteousness based on the law I was blameless" (Philippians 3:6).

But their fidelity to Mosaic law was quite shallow and external. As Jesus said, they pay "tithes of mint and dill and cummin, and have neglected the weightier things of the law: judgment and mercy and fidelity…" (Matthew 23:23). Our Lord compared them to whitewashed tombs that appear beautiful on the outside but inside are filled with every kind of filth (Matthew 23:27). Jesus' view of the Pharisees as hypocrites was well-known to everyone who followed him.

With this in mind, let's return to our passage. When Jesus said, "Let the one among you who is without sin cast the first stone," did he authorize an illegal stoning? If the Pharisees stoned the woman, could they convince the Romans that Jesus' words authorized them to break Roman law? On the other hand, if the Pharisees didn't stone the woman, they would implicitly show the crowd Jesus is right: they are sinners. Their trap for Jesus had swung around and trapped them. The elders were the first to realize their predicament and silently left (John 8:9). Truly, all who forsake the Lord are indeed confounded (Jeremiah 17:13).

John 8:51-58 - Who was the "Third Man" Who Visited Abraham? (September 18, 2015)

Whenever Scripture says something unexpected or difficult to understand, it usually is a sign something more is going on behind the passage. For example, have you ever noticed the strange turns in Jesus' conversation with the Jews about Abraham in John 8:51-58?

Jesus says whoever will keep my words will never see death (v. 51)

The Jews respond: "Are you greater than our father Abraham, who died?..." (v. 53)

Jesus later says: "Abraham your father rejoiced to see my day; he saw it and was glad." (v. 56)

The Jews respond: "You are not yet fifty years old and you have seen Abraham?" (v. 57)

Jesus says: "Amen, amen, I say to you, before Abraham came to be, I AM." (v. 58)

Then the Jews began to pick up stones to throw at Jesus.

What is going on here? Clearly, the Jews understood Jesus to have blasphemed. But why?

At first glance, it could have been Jesus' use of "I AM." As you know, God told Moses that His name is "I AM WHO AM." Is Jesus applying the divine name to himself? It seems so. However, that doesn't make sense in the context of the conversation. Jesus says Abraham "rejoiced to see my day." The Jews respond that He is not even 50 years old. Jesus responds "Before Abraham came to be..." the divine name. It doesn't make a lot of sense. Moreover, how is it that Abraham rejoiced to see Jesus' day? There's more going on than meets the eye.

One possible answer might be found in Abraham's mysterious visit in Genesis 18. One day, three men came to Abraham, who shows them hospitality and pays them reverence. One of the mysterious visitors says, "I will surely return to you about this time next year, and Sarah will then have a son" (Genesis 18:10). Sarah, Abraham's wife, laughs because they are too old. The visitor answers, "Is anything too marvelous for the LORD to do? At the appointed time … next year, I will return to you, and Sarah will have a son" (Genesis 18:14). One year later, Sarah gave birth to Isaac, which means "laughter." The Scripture says, "The LORD took note of Sarah as he had said he would; he did for her as he had promised. Sarah … bore Abraham a son in his old age, at the set time that God had stated" (Genesis 21:1-2). Was this the day, the birth of his son "laughter," that Abraham rejoiced?

What's curious is that the text is not at all clear who or what was this mysterious visitor. The chapter begins by saying the Lord [Yahweh] appeared to Abraham, and looking up he saw three men (Genesis 18:1). After overhearing one of the visitors say that she will give birth, Sarah laughed. In response, the text says, "But the LORD [Yahweh] said to Abraham: 'Why did Sarah laugh … Is anything too marvelous for the LORD to do? At the appointed time, about this time next year, I will return to you, and Sarah will have a son" (Genesis 18:13-14). Also, Genesis 18:22 says, "Then the men turned away from there and went toward Sodom, while Abraham was still standing before the Lord [Yahweh]." But there were three "men" who visited Abraham (Genesis 18:2) and only two angels came to Sodom (Genesis 19:1). Where was the third "man"? Apparently, the third "man" was the one still talking to Abraham, the Lord (Genesis 18:22). Our English translations say "Lord" in Genesis 18, but the Hebrew text gives the divine name YHWH ("I AM WHO AM").

Let's rewind back to our original passage in John 8. Jesus said Abraham "rejoiced to see my day." If this is the day of the miraculous birth of Isaac, then "my day" means the day of the mysterious visitor's return to Abraham and Sarah, who is YHWH ("I AM WHO AM"). If Abraham's visitation was a theophany (an appearance by God) then Jesus' application of the divine name fits perfectly with the whole discussion on Abraham. He visited Abraham. He is "I AM." It also explains why the Jews wanted to stone Jesus.

John 10:16 - Who are the 'Other Sheep" Jesus Says Belongs to Him? (Aug. 7, 2015)

Jesus makes a rather cryptic reference in John 10:16 that has sometimes baffled the casual Bible-reader. After speaking about how He will lay down his life for the sheep, Jesus says, "I have other sheep that do not belong to this fold. These also I must lead, and they will hear my voice, and there will be one flock, one shepherd."

Who are these "other sheep?"

Because the reference to "other sheep" seems to come out of thin air, not a few have attempted to capitalize on its vagueness. For example, the Mormons suggest that the "other sheep" were the fabled Nephites in the Americas! But there is no need to reach for such extravagant answers.

This verse contains a clue to the real identity of these "other sheep." Jesus says that these "other sheep … do not belong to this fold."

The word "fold" (Greek, *aule*) means a courtyard for animals. It is a gated area where the sheep can safely wander, being walled in from the wild. The "other sheep" are apparently outside the walled enclosure.

Jesus' reference to the Jews being sheep within a fold is quite apt. They were a people separate and distinct from the other nations because of the ceremonial law, which included ritual circumcision, dietary regulations, regulations on ritual cleanness, temple sacrifices and so on. Even the Jerusalem temple marked off the Jewish worshipers from gentiles.

The temple court was divided into the outer court of the gentiles and the inner court where Israelites alone could worship God and offer sacrifices, and a literal wall separated the two. The gates leading into the inner courts had signs posted warning gentiles that if they entered, they'd face the death penalty. If the Jews of the first century were sheep, the temple with its boundaries made them sheep in a fold. And this is not something that is bad. The Old Covenant was designed for the sanctification of Israel, so that they could be separated from paganism, purged of idolatry, and to prepare for the coming of the Messiah. And as we will soon see, once the Messiah had come and instituted the New Covenant, the division between Jew and gentile is removed.

Another clue that the "other sheep" refers to the gentiles is found in verse 15, where Jesus says, right before mentioning the "other sheep," that He will lay down His life for the sheep. Christ's death and the leading of the "other sheep" are associated together. Jesus makes a similar statement a few chapters later, when He says, "And when I am lifted up from the earth, I will draw everyone to myself" (John 12:32). Being "lifted up from the earth" refers to Christ's crucifixion (John 12:33). And what happens through Christ's death? "...I will draw everyone to myself." Christ's death will draw all people, Jews and gentiles, to Himself.

Elsewhere, Paul, alluding to the wall that separated the court of the gentiles from the inner court, says Christ's death destroyed the "wall of enmity" between Jews and gentiles, gathering both into one Body, the Church (Ephesians 2:14-16). The sheep who were once walled off are now part of one flock.

The Old Testament confirms that the Messiah and the New Covenant includes gentiles as well. For example, "On that day, the root of Jesse, set up as a signal for the nations, the Gentiles shall seek out, for his dwelling shall be glorious" (Isaiah 11:10). Isaiah also predicted that the Messiah, God's servant, would minister not only to Israel, but as a light to the gentiles as well: "It is too little, he says, for you to be my servant, to raise up the tribes of Jacob, and restore the survivors of Israel; I will make you a light to the nations, that my salvation may reach to the ends of the earth" (Isaiah 49:6).

So don't be sheepish about identifying the "other sheep" in John 10. There are no longer gates in the New Covenant; all people, both Jew and gentile, are welcome in.

John 20:21-23 - Did the Apostles Forgive Sins or Just Proclaim Forgiveness (May 1, 2015)

It's good to stick close to the words of Scripture to avoid distorting its meaning. But sometimes focusing too much on one aspect of a passage can also distort its meaning. A good example of this kind of distortion can be seen in a very important text where Jesus gives the Apostles the authority to forgive sins in John 20:21-23:

"[Jesus] said to them again, 'Peace be with you. As the Father has sent me, so I send you.' And when he had said this, he breathed on them and said to them, 'Receive the Holy Spirit. Whose sins you forgive are forgiven them, and whose sins you retain are retained.'"

I frequently use this text to explain to non-Catholics the sacrament of confession. It's a great passage because it is so simple. The text speaks for itself. But I've learned that the plain meaning of a text isn't always so plain to non-Catholics, especially those who believe in something called "eternal security."

According to this belief, once someone becomes a Christian, their entrance into heaven is guaranteed; there is nothing a Christian can do to lose his salvation. Once he is saved, he is always saved. Confession, therefore, is unnecessary because all of one's sins (past, present and future) are already forgiven.

If this were true, however, why would Jesus give the apostles the authority to forgive sins? Those who hold to "eternal security" say Christ wasn't bestowing upon the apostles any special authority; rather, he was telling them that they were to proclaim to those who are "saved" that all their sins have already been forgiven and to those who refused to be "saved" that all their sins remain upon them.

How do they do this? James McCarthy in his anti-Catholic work, "The Gospel According to Rome," appeals to the Greek words translated "forgive" and "retained" in John 20:22-23 and points out that these words indicate a past completed action. In fact, the *New American Standard Bible* (a Protestant translation that sticks closely to the literal sense of the text) translates John 20:22-23 as: "If you forgive the sins of any, their sins have been forgiven them; if you retain the sins of any, they have been retained."

All is well and good. But here's where the interpretive twist comes in: McCarthy and those who believe in "eternal security" then argue that these sins must already have been forgiven or retained before the apostles said or did anything. In other words, the apostles aren't forgiving sins, but only proclaiming to Christians that their sins have already been forgiven back when they were first saved. Presto! Confession vanishes.

But is this really what John 20:22-23 is saying?

I must confess that this argument stumped me when I first began sharing and explaining the faith, until one day I looked up the passage in a Protestant reference work designed to aid Protestant scholars in translating the Bible. What it showed me was that by focusing so much attention on the verbs in John 20:22-23, they had missed the proverbial "forest through the trees."

What did they miss? They forgot that Jesus' statement is conditional. He says *"If* you forgive the sins of any … *If* you retain the sins of any …" What this means is that when the condition is met (i.e. the apostles forgive/retain sins) then the following result occurs (the sins have been forgiven/retained). The forgiveness of sins, therefore, did not take place before the apostles' actions, but it occurs *when* the Apostles forgive or retain sins. In other words, Jesus is investing the apostles with the authority to actually forgive sins.

We can see this investment of authority one verse earlier when "... Jesus breathed on them and said, 'Receive the Holy Spirit.'" What does this breathing mean? In Scripture, it shows the bestowal of new life (Genesis 2:7, Ezekiel 37:9-14). This gift of the Holy Spirit empowers the apostles to carry out their mission of mercy and forgiveness.

John 21:15-17 - When a Fisherman Became A Shepherd (June 24, 2016)

Where did Jesus make Peter the visible head of His Church? Most people would turn to Matthew 16:17-19, where Jesus changes Simon's name to Peter and says "... upon this rock I will build My Church." It is also the passage where Jesus gives Peter the "keys of the kingdom of heaven" and the power to bind and loose.

If you look closely at this passage, however, you'll notice that everything is in the future tense, "... I will build My Church ... I will give the keys of the kingdom of heaven ..." Matthew 16:17-19 is the promise given to Peter, but where does Jesus actually fulfill this promise? The answer is John 21:15-17:

> "When they had finished breakfast, Jesus said to Simon Peter, 'Simon, son of John, do you love me

> more than these?' He said to him, 'Yes, Lord, you know that I love you.' He said to him, 'Feed my lambs.' He then said to him a second time, 'Simon, son of John, do you love me?' He said to him, 'Yes, Lord, you know that I love you.' He said to him, 'Tend my sheep.' He said to him the third time, 'Simon, son of John, do you love me?' Peter was distressed that he had said to him a third time, 'Do you love me?' and he said to him, 'Lord, you know everything; you know that I love you.' (Jesus) said to him, 'Feed my sheep.'"

If you've ever appealed to this verse to show the founding of the papacy, your non-Catholic friend might have responded, "You're making too much out of this verse. All that is going on is that Simon Peter denied Jesus three times and Jesus is restoring him with a three-fold affirmation of love. That's all."

It's true that John 21:15-17 is restoring Peter from his threefold denial of Christ before the crucifixion, but what is often missed is that Jesus had already spoken about this moment before his Passion. In Luke 22:31–32, Jesus said to Simon Peter:

> "Simon, Simon, behold Satan has demanded to sift all of you like wheat, but I have prayed that your own faith may not fail; and once you have turned back, you must strengthen your brothers."

There is a lot going on in this short passage, so let's unpack what our Lord is saying. First, Jesus says Satan has "demanded to sift all of you like wheat." When Jesus says "all of you," who is he talking about? He's talking about the Apostles. The Apostles were to be scattered, and they were during Christ's Passion.

Second, Jesus prays specifically for Simon Peter. This is the only time Jesus is said to pray for a specific person, but why would Jesus need to pray for anyone? (He is God, after all.) Jesus prays so that we would know what is on his heart. In this case, he wants us to know that it is his will that Peter's own faith will not fail and that once Peter has "turned back," he must strengthen his brothers. Peter turns back in John 21:15-17 when he affirms Christ with a three-fold confession of love for his three-fold denial.

Third, what does it mean to "strengthen your brothers?" Who are Simon Peter's brothers? Certainly, all Christians are brothers (Matthew 23:8), but in this context the only other people mentioned are the rest of the Apostles, of whom Satan has demanded to "sift like wheat." Jesus has prayed, and so it will happen, that once Simon Peter has "turned back" after his threefold denial, it is he who will become the source of unity among his brother apostles.

With this in mind, let's turn back to John 21:15-17 and ask ourselves this question: "How is Simon Peter going to be that source of unity?" The answer is that he will unify Christ's flock (apostles and all believers) as a shepherd. He will do all the things a shepherd does for his flock, lead it, guard it, and most of all keep it together. Jesus prayed, and so it is.

The Acts of the Apostles

Acts 5:35-39 - Christ was Killed; Why weren't His Followers Dispersed? (April 4, 2016)

When Peter and the apostles were brought before the Sanhedrin in Acts 5, a rabbi stood up and ordered the apostles to be removed from the room. The rabbi was Gamaliel.

Many of us might not be familiar with Gamaliel, but we should be. He is among the most revered sages in Judaism. He's so revered that Jewish literature says, "When he died the honor of the Torah ceased, and purity and piety became extinct" (Soṭah 15:18).

After the apostles had cleared the room, Gamaliel said this:

"Fellow Israelites, be careful what you are about to do to these men. Some time ago, Theudas appeared, claiming to be someone important, and about four hundred men joined him, but he was killed, and all those who were loyal to him were disbanded and came to nothing. After him came Judas the Galilean at the time of the census. He also drew people after him, but he too perished and all who were loyal to him were scattered. So now I tell you, have nothing to do with these men, and let them go. For if this endeavor or this activity is of human origin, it will destroy itself. But if it comes from God, you will not be able to destroy them; you may even find yourselves fighting against God" (Acts 5:35-39).

Jesus enters Jerusalem with his apostles in this 14th century work by Duccio. The revered Jewish rabbi Gamaliel prophesied that

Jesus' apostles would disband, unless Jesus' movement "comes from God."

Gamaliel's advice is perfectly in line with what he experienced during the first century, when all expected the messiah to come. Charismatic leaders arose and were cut down. Theudas was killed by the prefect Fadus around AD 44-46. Judas led a violent tax revolt in AD 6. Both had large followings and both movements disappeared after their leaders' death. When Gamaliel gave this advice, it was almost 20 years after Christ's crucifixion. These followers would soon disperse … or so one would think.

Fifty years later, the Jewish historian Josephus records a short passage about Jesus in his work, *Antiquity of the Jews*. At the end of the passage, he notes, "And the tribe of Christians, so named from him, are not extinct at this day" [Antiquities, 18, 3, 3]. This undoubtedly was a surprising fact for Josephus because he, like Gamaliel above, knew the first century pattern for pseudo-messiahs. He records such figures as Judas ben Hezekiah, Simon of Peraea, Athronges the shepherd, the unnamed Egyptian false prophet, an unknown Samaritan prophet, Menahem, John of Gischala, Simon bar Giora, and Jonathan the weaver. All of these leaders gained a following, were killed, and their movement came to nothing. But Jesus' followers were still around. How strange!

Another person writing not long after Josephus notes the same oddity. This person is not Jewish, but pagan. In fact, he is the Roman senator and historian Tacitus (AD ca. 56 – ca. 117), who wrote:

> "Nero fastened the guilt and inflicted the most exquisite tortures on a class hated for their

abominations, called Christians by the populace. Christus, from whom the name had its origin, suffered the extreme penalty during the reign of Tiberius at the hands of one of our procurators, Pontius Pilatus, and a most mischievous superstition, thus checked for the moment, again broke out not only in Judaea, the first source of the evil, but even in Rome" [Annuals 15:44].

As you can see, Tacitus believed that Christ's death under "Pontius Pilatus" ought to have stopped the movement. He, too, knew that once the leader is executed, his followers have no reason to continue. But oddly enough, Christianity was checked only for a moment, but it again broke out and spread from Judaea even to Rome.

What Gamaliel, Josephus and Tacitus didn't ask was the obvious question: Why? Why didn't Christianity disappear after its leader's death? Josephus records the reason: "They report that he had appeared to them three days after his crucifixion and that he was alive…" (Arabic version).

The leader of the Christians isn't dead. He's alive, enthroned, and reigning at the right hand of the Father. This is why the Church is still alive and well and spreading over the Earth. Gamaliel's advice, therefore, was indeed wise. Our faith does indeed come from God and therefore it cannot be destroyed.

Acts 7:59 - When the Cat's Away: The Background to St. Stephen's Martyrdom (Oct. 16, 2014)

Scripture often takes us on some unexpected turns. Many times these surprises are due to the changing social backdrop that are unknown to us readers, but well known to the Scripture's original audience.

For example, why did the Jews lack the authority to execute Jesus, but only a few years later in the Acts of the Apostles, are they able to execute St. Stephen? What changed? A quick look "behind the Bible" reveals something very interesting behind the contexts of these two deaths.

Christ's death took placed under the reign of Pontius Pilate (A.D. 26-36), the fifth prefect of Judea. Under the Roman provincial system, the Roman senate had jurisdiction over the peaceful providences of the empire. For providences that were less stable and needed closer supervision, however, they appointed a procurator who, with Roman troops at his disposal, was to ensure order.

Under the Roman procurator, the Sanhedrin was able to exercise a measure of freedom. One freedom they did not have was the power to execute; only Roman authorities could administer capital punishment. This is why the Jews had to secure Pilate's approval and hand Jesus over to the Romans to be executed by crucifixion (John 18:31).

What Happened to Pilate?

The last we hear about Pilate in the New Testament is when Christ's disciples asked Pilate for permission to take down Our

Lord's body (Mark 15:43-44, Luke 23:52, John 19:38). After that, Pilate disappears from the pages of the New Testament, but not from history.

According to the first century Jewish historian, Flavius Josephus, Pilate was anything but a friend to the Jews whom he ruled. Instead of securing peace and tranquility for those in Judea, he caused disturbances and violence. Pilate's ultimate downfall came when he order the slaughter of a large number of Samaritans. The Samaritans sent an embassy to Vitellius, who was the president of Syria, and accused Pilate of murder. Josephus tells us:

> "So Vitellius sent Marcellus, a friend of his, to take care of the affairs of Judea, and ordered Pilate to go to Rome, to answer before the emperor to the accusations of the Jews. So Pilate, when he had tarried 10 years in Judea, made haste to Rome, and this in obedience to the orders of Vitellius, which he durst not contradict; but before he could get to Rome Tiberius was dead" (Antiquity of the Jews, 18, 4, 2).

Pilate's recall to Rome, around A.D. 36, created a temporary power-vacuum or disorder within Judea. And as the old childhood rhyme says, "When the cat is away, the mice will play." This period between procurators would have allowed the Jewish citizens the opportunity to carry out capital punishment without any real fear of Roman reprisal, and A.D. 36 fits perfectly with the timeframe in which St. Stephen was stoned to death.

This is one of those unexpected turns of Scripture where, if one didn't know the political background behind St. Stephen's stoning, it would appear that his stoning was inconsistent with what we know about Roman rule and its prohibition on non-Roman executions. Instead, his stoning makes perfect sense in terms of the social-political background at this time.

If there is anything this teaches us, it is that when we read Scripture, we ought to approach the text with a certain amount of intellectual humility. We don't know everything, and what we don't know can make things appear odd or out of place when in fact what Scripture records is perfectly true and accurate.

Acts 18:3 - No Town Like His Hometown: How St. Paul's Shaped His Life (August 22, 2014)

God never commands the impossible — although he may command the very difficult.

In all cases, God provides for our needs, and His providence guides and shapes us. There is no clearer example of God's providential care and preparation of an individual in the New Testament than St. Paul.

After his conversion to Christ, Paul was a powerful instrument for God to spread the Gospel, not only through his various missionary journeys, but also through his writings. No other single New Testament author wrote as much as Paul. His writings make up more than 30 percent of the books of the New Testament.

But how did God prepare Paul to spread the Gospel? One way is found in a seemingly mundane biographical detail: the place of

Paul's birth, Tarsus of Cilicia in Asia Minor (in modern-day Turkey).

Paul's birth in Tarsus shaped and prepared Paul to be the Apostle to the gentiles in three important ways.

First, Tarsus enabled Paul to receive a superior Jewish education. We know that Paul studied Judaism at the feet of rabbi Gamaliel I (Acts 22:3), a very respected rabbi who is still revered by Jews today. Education was costly in that students had to support themselves during their training. How did Paul support himself? He was a tentmaker (Acts 18:3). This was no accident because Tarsus was considered a center for tent-making. The sheep's wool at Tarsus was particularly well-suited for tent making. Moreover, tent-making was an important and potentially lucrative trade. Tarsus, therefore, supplied Paul with the means to study under Gamaliel and perhaps even fund some of his extensive missionary journeys.

Second, Tarsus also exposed Paul to different cultures. Did you ever wonder why Paul seemed so comfortable debating the pagan Greek philosophers in Athens (Acts 17)? Tarsus again provides an answer. Like the city of St. Louis last century, Tarsus was a gateway city between East and West. This interchange of cultures made it an ideal location for pagan education, including instruction in Stoic philosophy.

At one time, the schools in Tarsus were considered on par or even surpassed those in Athens. As a native of Tarsus, Paul likely rubbed elbows with Stoic philosophers on the streets and became familiar with their view of life, so when the Stoic and Epicurean philosophers in Athens wanted to dialogue with Paul (Acts 17:17-18), he was ready and willing.

The third and perhaps greatest gift Tarsus gave to Paul was his Roman citizenship. Roman citizenship was prized throughout the ancient Roman empire because it granted special legal protection under Roman law. Citizens could not be bound or whipped (scourged), nor could they be put to death except when found guilty of treason — and even then they were allowed to appeal to Caesar.

If you weren't born a Roman citizen, becoming a citizen wasn't easy; you would either have to serve honorably in the Roman military for 25 years or more, or you would have to buy the privilege, which was very expensive (see Acts 22:28). Paul was neither born in Rome nor served in its military, nor did he buy his citizenship. How did he become a Roman citizen? He was born in Tarsus.

Tarsus was a favored city of the Roman Empire long before Paul. In 67 BC, Pompey made Tarsus the capital of the Roman province of Cilicia, and Mark Antony, who was in control over the eastern provinces, declared Tarsus a city free in 42 BC. Caesar Augustus, whose friend and teacher was from Tarsus, favored the city by granting it exemption from imperial taxes. St. Paul's birth in Tarsus gave him Roman citizenship, which he skillfully used to preach the Gospel to audiences who otherwise could not read, and his citizenship in one instance even saved his life through appeal to Caesar (Acts 25:10-11).

St. Paul could have been born in any city in the ancient world, but God providentially chose Tarsus, a city that supplied Paul with the skills and resources he needed to answer God's call. How has God providentially shaped your life? What skills and resources has God's providence provided you to answer His call?

Acts 19:8-12 - No Luck Evangelizing? Try St. Paul Method (March 21, 2016)

Catholics face lots of opposition in the media and from the culture, and it is easy to get discouraged, especially when good and holy endeavors don't work out the way we planned. If the Acts of the Apostles teaches anything, it is that God's way is always the best way, even if means taking a step back to move that much more forward.

It's difficult to imagine the opposition St. Paul faced after his conversion to Christianity. Practically no one had heard the Gospel and many opposed it without a hearing. If there was anyone in the world who should have been discouraged, it was St. Paul. But the apostle didn't get discouraged because, as he writes in Philippians 4:11-12, "…I have learned, in whatever situation I find myself, to be self-sufficient. I know indeed how to live in humble circumstances; I know also how to live with abundance. In every circumstance and in all things I have learned the secret of being well fed and of going hungry, of living in abundance and of being in need."

What was the secret? Paul knew that in whatever circumstance he found himself, it was part of God's plan. His faith and hope pulled him through.

Take, for example, what happened to Paul in Acts 19:8-12. Paul had left his friend Apollos in Corinth and traveled down to Ephesus (Acts 19:1), where he found some disciples of John the Baptist — not exactly the best situation, but they were able to receive the Holy Spirit (Acts 19:5-6). Now he was ready to evangelize! Luke records that Paul entered into the synagogue, "...and for three months debated boldly with persuasive arguments about the kingdom of God." But after three months of passionate and persuasive arguments, no converts. In fact, some unbelievers began disparaged Christianity before the assembly. Paul had hit a dead end.

Instead of shaking the dust from his sandals and moving on to another town that was more open-minded, "he withdrew and took his disciples with him and began to hold daily discussions in the lecture hall of Tyrannus" (Acts 19:9). A little background behind this verse really shows how much of a step back it was. The synagogue was really Paul's home turf. Whenever he entered a city to evangelize, he headed for the synagogue. Remember that before his conversion, Paul was an incredibly well-educated Pharisee. But he was forced to abandon the "home-turf advantage" of the synagogue and move to a pagan lecture hall. We don't know anything about Tyrannus. He may have taught rhetoric and the hall Paul moved to was where he gave his lectures.

The good news was the hall probably accommodated a lot of people. The bad news comes by way of a Syriac manuscript that adds a comment for this verse: Paul lectured "from the 5th hour until the 10th" (that is, the time before and after noon). In other words, the only time the hall was available was when no one wanted to use it, during the hottest part of the day. Not exactly the ideal conditions for evangelism.

One would think that this new arrangement wouldn't last very long. No one would come in the heat to a pagan lecture hall to talk about religion. Against all humanly expectations, it turned out to be an incredible success, and Paul continued this way for two whole years with the result "… that all the inhabitants of the province of Asia heard the word of the Lord, Jews and Greeks alike. So extraordinary were the mighty deeds God accomplished at the hands of Paul that when face cloths or aprons that touched his skin were applied to the sick, their diseases left them and the evil spirits came out of them" (Acts 19:10-12).

Had Paul continued where he was comfortable, he might have won a few people to the faith, but his willingness to step out of his evangelistic comfort zone and accept whatever situation God gave him resulted in an explosion conversions. Paul's secret to overcoming adversity is knowing that when you are doing God's will, the worst circumstances can become the most fruitful situations.

The Epistles of St. Paul

Romans 4:1-4 - Was Abraham a Jew or a Gentile? (July 13, 2015)

Discussions with non-Catholics often center on the role of faith and good works. Many non-Catholics believe we are made right with God through faith alone, and to prove this commonly appeal to what Paul says about Abraham in Romans 4:1-5: "If Abraham was justified on the basis of his works, he has reason to boast; but this was not so in the sight of God. For what does the scripture say? 'Abraham believed God, and it was credited to him as righteousness'" (Romans 4:2-3).

It seems as though Paul is saying Abraham was made right with God by faith alone apart from anything he did (i.e., works). Is this true?

What non-Catholics often miss, though, is that Paul's appeal to Abraham is part of an argument he is making against a group known as the Judaizers, and that Paul's point is much more profound than they realize.

Who were the Judaizers? They were Jewish converts to Christianity who believed it was necessary for gentile Christian converts to first be circumcised and follow the Mosaic Law in order to become Christian (Acts 15:5). For them, circumcision was necessary for salvation (Acts 15:1). Not only was it necessary, but they also believed that by being circumcised and following the Old Testament ceremonial law (which Paul sometimes calls "the works of the law") they could live immorally and still escape God's wrath (Romans 2:3).

Paul takes on the Judaizers' presumption in a number of ways in Romans 2-3. He argues that all people, Jew and gentile, will be judged according to their deeds (Romans 2:2-11) and that merely possessing the Ten Commandment without doing them will not make you right with God (Romans 2:12-16). And he also argues that the moral law, being faithful to God from the heart, is superior to the ceremonial law (i.e., circumcision) (Romans 2:17-29), and that even some of the circumcised (whom the Judaizers believe are righteous in virtue of their circumcision) were condemned in Scripture as unrighteous and wicked (Romans 3:9-19). Finally, Paul argues that God makes no distinction between Jews and gentiles (circumcised and uncircumcised) because both have sinned and both are freely justified by God's grace through faith (Romans 3:21-31). God is not partial (Romans 2:11). God's doesn't play favorites.

This sets up Paul's remarkable argument about Abraham in Romans 4:1-5. God gave Abraham the covenant of circumcision and the Judaizers prided themselves of being the children of Abraham.

Paul states, "If Abraham was justified on the basis of his works (i.e., circumcision and the Mosaic Law), he has reason to boast; but this was not so in the sight of God." Then Paul appeals to Genesis 15:6, which says that "Abraham believed God, and it was credited to him as righteousness." What's remarkable about Paul's argument is that he shows that Abraham was declared righteous before God before he received the covenant of circumcision. God calls Abraham righteous in Genesis 15:6, but Abraham didn't receive the covenant of circumcision until two chapters later in Genesis 17, some 29 years later. What does this mean?

Paul asks, "Under what circumstances was it credited? Was he circumcised or not? He was not circumcised, but uncircumcised" (Romans 4:10). In other words, Abraham was righteous by faith as a gentile (i.e., someone uncircumcised). This clinches Paul's argument. It wasn't circumcision that made Abraham acceptable to God or righteous, but his faith. If that's true for Abraham, it's also true for all gentiles who come to faith in Jesus. They too are made acceptable to God by faith.

According to Paul, Abraham is the father of the uncircumcised (i.e., the gentiles) who believe, and also the father of the circumcised who "…follow the path of faith that our father Abraham walked while still uncircumcised" (Romans 4:11).

Romans 4:1-11 is not arguing that we are made acceptable to God by faith alone (apart from any good deeds we do after baptism), but that it is faith, not circumcision, that makes all people, Jews and gentiles, right in God's sight.

Galatians 3:26-29 - Who is the Blessed Offspring of Abraham? (October 30, 2015)

We're familiar with the Church's teaching on the body of Christ, but how many of us really appreciate what it means to *be* the body of Christ? In my book, *Making Sense of Mary,* I explored the surprising implications of this doctrine in prophecies about Christ and His mother. Before we explore one of these prophecies, the seed of Abraham through which all the nations will be blessed, we need to remind ourselves how radical our union with Christ truly is.

There is no better place to start than St. Paul's conversion (Acts 9:4, 22:7, and 26:14). Paul encounters the risen Lord on his way to Damascus. Jesus says to him, "Saul, Saul, why are you persecuting me?" Jesus' words to St. Paul is interesting. Jesus did not say, "Saul, Saul, why are you persecuting my followers?" or "… persecuting those who have a personal relationship with me?" No. He said, "…why are you persecuting *me*?" To persecute members of Christ's body is to persecute Christ, the head. As someone once said, "When you strike the toe, the head complains."

Our unity with Christ is so radical that Christ associates us with Himself in such an intimate way that he uses the analogy of a head to its body. Christ's words made a great impact on the saint's theology. Indeed, no other New Testament writer speaks as much about the mystical body of Christ as St. Paul, and his understanding impacts everything, including Old Testament prophecies. In fact, it's almost impossible to make sense of some of Paul's teachings without taking Christ as Head and Body into account.

Take, for example, Paul's teaching about God's promise that through Abraham's offspring (literally "seed") all the nations will be blessed (Genesis 22:18). Paul is emphatic that the "seed" spoken of in this prophesy does not refer to many descendants, but only to one individual. He makes this point in a very unusual way in Galatians 3:16: "Now the promises were made to Abraham and to his descendant. It does not say, 'And to descendants,' as referring to many, but as referring to one, 'And to your descendant,' who is

Christ." This is strange, because in Hebrew, the word for "descendant" (seed) is singular, but it's a collective singular. It's singular, but it refers to many. We use the same convention in English; all of the children of Abraham are referred to using the singular "offspring" or "seed," not "offsprings" or "seeds."

Scholars have been scratching their heads why Paul would make such a strained point. But given the biblical background of St. Paul and his understanding of how intimate our union is with Christ, our head, it's not strained at all.

However, Paul doesn't stop there. Later on, he says the following: "For through faith you are all children of God in Christ Jesus. For all of you who were baptized into Christ have clothed yourselves with Christ … for you are all one in Christ Jesus. And if you belong to Christ, then you are Abraham's descendant, heirs according to the promise" (Galatians 3:26-29).

Wait a second! How many *are* Abraham's descendant or seed? In Galatians 3:16, Paul insisted it referred only to one individual, but here he says it refers to many people, those "baptized into Christ." In fact, the word Paul insists is singular in Galatians 3:16 is also singular in Galatians 3:26-29. Well, which is it Paul? Is Christ alone Abraham's seed or are Christians Abraham's seed? Paul's answer seems to be "yes." Christ is Abraham's individual singular seed both as Head and Body.

Why bring up that the "seed" is singular? I think Paul is saying that the singular collective was a good way to express Christ as Head and Body. The singular word expresses only one individual, and yet at the same time it expresses many within that word just as "…we, though many, are one body in Christ" (Romans 12:5). Christ's union with us is so profound that even biblical prophecies about the messiah have reference to us, the Church. Think about this union the next time you receive Communion (1 Corinthians 10:17).

Ephesians 2:15 - Getting into Trouble with the Law (September 16, 2016)

The relationship between the Old Testament and Christian doctrine can be puzzling at times, especially when it comes to the Old Testament legislation known as the Law.

Why is it that some parts of the Law of Moses are still binding, while other parts are not? Have you ever wondered why we follow the Ten Commandments, yet are not still required to circumcise? Why the prohibition of homosexual acts is still in force, but sacrificing animals is not?

Adding to the confusion, the New Testament even seems to contradict itself in some places regarding the Law. For example, Jesus tells a man, "If you wish to enter into life, keep the commandments" (Matt. 19:17), yet Paul says that Jesus abolished "… the law with its legal claims" (Ephesians 2:15). What gives? Is the Church arbitrarily picking and choosing which parts of the Law of Moses to keep and ignoring the rest?

Yet there's a simple answer to this conundrum: not all of the laws given by Moses are the same. In fact, the Law of Moses is comprised of three different types of laws, which St. Thomas Aquinas identified as the "ceremonial" law, the "moral" law, and the "juridical" law. Each of these types were meant to regulate different areas of life. As such, some types of law can change, while others cannot. Let's look at each type:

The *ceremonial law* was meant to regulate Old Covenant worship. It included things such as cleanliness laws, kosher diet, circumcision, animal sacrifices and feast days. Paul calls the ceremonial law "shadows of things to come" (Colossians 2:17); they were figures that pointed toward or foreshadowed Christ. But once Christ had come and established the New Covenant, the ceremonial law became obsolete (Hebrews 8:13). This is why Christians no longer are required to abstain from pork, be circumcised, offer animal sacrifices, and so on.

The *moral law* regulated how one ought to live. The moral law came into existence long before Moses received the Ten Commandments on Sinai, as it is inscribed, Paul tells us, in nature itself. By observing how things in nature are ordered toward certain ends, one can know in a general way what is and what is not moral. This is why Paul says that "… the gentiles, who have not the law, do by nature those things that are of the law" (Roman 2:14).

The gentiles didn't know the Ten Commandments, but they knew certain general moral tenants, albeit imperfectly. The Ten Commandments made explicit what could be known imperfectly through nature. The rest of the moral laws in the Old Testament simply unpack what had been given in the Decalogue. Because the moral law is rooted in nature and made explicit through the Ten Commandments, its substance can never change and is always binding.

The *juridical law* was meant to "shape the state of that people according to justice and equity." Probably the easiest way to understand the juridical law is that it applied the principles of the moral law to concrete situations. For example, Deuteronomy 22:8 says that anyone building a new house must put a barrier (parapet) around the roof. People used to walk across flat-roofed houses, and this law was meant to prevent injuries due to the owners' negligence. Because lifestyles change (i.e., people don't normally use roofs as walkways), the law is no longer in effect, although its underlying principles (i.e., that it's wrong to cause injuries through negligence) is still in force.

As you can see, not everything in the Law of Moses is the same. The moral law can never be substantially changed, while the ceremonial law, which pointed toward Christ, can become obsolete. The juridical law no longer applies, but its underlying principles, which are rooted in the moral law, are still binding. So the next time someone accuses Christians of cherry-picking commandments, it might prove helpful to explain the three types of the Law of Moses.

Philippians 1:27-30 - Onward Christian Soldiers of Philippi (March 9, 2017)

If you're like me, you usually skip over the introductory remarks in your Bible and go straight to reading a biblical text. After all, do we really need to know all the details about the places to whom Paul wrote? As tempting as this shortcut might be, you could miss out on several valuable insights.

For example, Paul's letter to the Philippians is a good example of how knowing the historical background of Philippi can help illuminate Paul's message.

Philippi was named after Philip II of Macedon, the father of Alexander the Great, who defeated the Thracians and took the city in 356 B.C. In 31 B.C., Octavian defeated Antony and Cleopatra at Actium and rebuilt Philippi, turning it into a military outpost. By placing retired soldiers in Philippi, Octavian shrewdly ensured the city's loyalty to Rome. As a military colony, retired army veterans enjoyed the benefits of being Roman citizens and other civic privileges.

If you read Paul's letter to the Philippians with this military background in mind, you'll catch all sorts of references and allusions to military service. After all, what better way to explain contending for the faith to a military colony than to appeal to the life they knew best?

Take, for example, Philippians 1:27-30. Paul writes:

> "Only let your manner of life be worthy of the gospel of Christ, so that whether I come and see you or am absent, I may hear of you that you stand firm in one spirit, with one mind striving side by side for the faith of the gospel, and not frightened in anything by your opponents. This is a clear omen to them of their destruction, but of your salvation, and that from God. For it has been granted to you that for the sake of Christ you should not only believe in him but also suffer for

his sake, engaged in the same conflict which you saw and now hear to be mine."

This passage is riddled with military ideas. Like an army, Christians are to stand firm, united in one spirit, fighting "side by side" for the faith of the Gospel, and not being frightened by the enemy.

It's interesting that Paul insists that Christians should fight "side by side." This was already an old military tactic. The ancient Greek author Onasander counseled generals to station their solders in pairs with friends standing next to friends and brothers standing next to brothers so that when danger comes the soldiers will fight more recklessly for the friend or brother beside him. Paul seems to have the same thing in mind with Christians. We are like soldiers standing side by side with our brothers and sisters contending for the faith.

Another ancient military idea was that generals should lead by example. Paul likewise offers himself as an example for the Christians in Philippi. He says that both he and the Christians at Phillippi were engaging in the same battle, "…which you saw and now hear to be mine."

Elsewhere, he encourages them, like good soldiers to "… [d]o all things without grumbling or questioning" (Philippians 2:14).

Paul even speaks of Epaphroditus as a heroic soldier:

> "I have thought it necessary to send to you Epaphroditus my brother and fellow worker and fellow soldier, and your messenger and minister to my need, for he has been longing for you all, and has been distressed because you heard that he was

> ill … So receive him in the Lord with all joy; and honor such men, for he nearly died for the work of Christ, risking his life to complete your service to me" (Philippians 2:25-26, 30).

Epaphroditus is described by Paul as a "fellow soldier" who risked his life to carry out his service for Paul. He therefore exhorts the Church in Philippi to "honor such men" just as soldiers are honored for going beyond and above the call of duty.

These are only a few of dozens of references in Philippians that take on a deeper meaning when looked at from a military perspective. Read it for yourself and see what other references you can find.

1 Corinthian 5:21 - "If He Makes Himself An Offering for Sin..." (April 7, 2017)

It was once said that the Bible is so simple and plainly set forth that even a child can understand it. Yes, Scripture does contain plain and easy-to-understand teachings, but there are also passages in which the authors assume that the audience understands the Old Testament background. Take as an example the seemingly simple teaching in 1 Corinthians 5:21, which reads:

> "For our sake he [the Father] made him [Jesus] to be sin who did not know sin, so that we might become the righteousness of God in him."

Was Jesus made "sin" on the cross, and what does that mean? Some non-Catholics have proposed that God saw the sins of humanity when he looked upon Jesus on the cross and vented his wrath upon them. But laying down one's life for another is the greatest act of love, and Christ's death on the cross is the greatest manifestation of God's love (John 10:11-12, 15:13-14, cf. Romans 5:8-9). It wasn't something detestable.

Why then does it say Christ was "made to be sin"? The early Church fathers knew that this phrase was deeply rooted in the Old Testament terminology concerning sacrifice. As Cyril of Alexandria wrote:

> "Thus Christ became a victim 'for our sins according to the Scriptures.' For this reason, we say that he was named sin ... For we do not say that Christ became a sinner, far from it, but being just, or rather in actuality justice, for he did not know sin, the Father made him a victim for the sins of the world. 'He was counted among the wicked' (Isaiah 53:12)" (Letter 41.10)

Augustine dives further into the Old Testament background:

> "And because he became the sacrifice for sin, offering himself as a holocaust on the cross of his passion ... the very same victims, the very same beasts which were presented to be immolated for sins, and in whose blood that blood was prefigured, these the Law calls sins, to such an extent that in certain passages [Leviticus 4:4, 15, 24, 29, and 33] it has been written thus, that priests, about to immolate, place their hands over the head of sin, that is, over the head of the victim

to be immolated for sin. Therefore such a 'sin,' that is, a sacrifice for sin, did our Lord Jesus Christ become, 'who knew not sin'" [Tract. in John 41.6].

To be "made sin," according to Old Testament terminology, is to be made a sin offering. But where in the Old Testament did we ever hear about someone making himself an offering for sin? The answer is found only a few verses earlier from the same passage cited by St. Cyril above, Isaiah 53:10.

Isaiah 52:13-53:12 is known as the "Suffering Servant" passage, and it makes marvelous reading for Lent and Holy Week. Speaking of this Suffering Servant who will be "bruised for our offenses" and although righteous "counted among the wicked" it says in verse 10: "… If he gives his life as an offering for sin, he shall see his descendants in a long life, and the will of the LORD shall be accomplished through him."

Just like the whole of the Suffering Servant oracle, it says so many surprising things. First, it speaks of the Servant "giving his life as an offering for sin." Second, even though he is to give his life for sin, Isaiah says that "we shall see his descendants in a long life." This refers to the Church, the members of his Body. But notice that although he is "cut off from the land of living" (Isaiah 53:8) he nevertheless "… shall see his descendants in a long life." One thing about sacrificial offerings, they don't continue to live after they've been offered, yet the sacrifice of the Suffering Servant is different: He lives to see the lives of his descendants.

This Lenten season, make it a point to read Isaiah 52-53 and see how Christ became "sin" so that we may be the righteousness of God in him.

1 Corinthians 15:3 - Discovering early evidence for the resurrection (May 15, 2014)

How many times have you seen cable programs that call into question the roots of Christianity? Usually, these programs try to gain viewers by attacking the basis for a recent religious holy day. At Christmas, they attack Christ's divinity. At Easter, they attack the resurrection. But what most viewers don't know is that nearly all of these seemingly new claims are really quite old and many of them have been discussed, debunked, and discarded by scholars in the field.

One common charge is that the data found in the New Testament was written too long after the fact to be reliable. Therefore, the claim of Christ's resurrection, for example, is more of a pious hope than a historical fact. But is this so? How should a Catholic respond to this claim?

There are several solid responses, but one of the most fascinating can be found by looking deeper into the historical background of 1 Corinthians 15:3-8, in which St. Paul recounts for the Church in Corinth a list of eyewitnesses to the risen Christ.

1 Corinthian 15:3-8 reads:

> "For I handed on to you as of first importance what I also received: that Christ died for our sins in accordance with the scriptures; that he was buried; that he was raised on the third day in accordance with the scriptures; that he appeared to Kephas, then to the Twelve. After that, he appeared to more than five hundred brothers at once, most of whom are still living, though some have fallen asleep. After that he appeared to James, then to all the apostles. Last of all, as to one born abnormally, he appeared to me."

How early is this testimony? Most scholars (Catholic, Protestant, and secular) date 1 Corinthians quite early, roughly A.D. 53-57. If the generally acknowledged date of Christ's resurrection is A.D. 30, then Paul's list of eyewitnesses would be only 23 to 27 years removed from the actual event. This is a remarkably short period of time, especially in comparison to pagan histories that were written decades — or even centuries — later. Indeed, 1 Corinthians was written so close to the resurrection that in verse 5, Paul mentions that most of the five hundred who saw the risen Christ were still alive!

But there is more to the story. Paul stated that this list of eyewitnesses is something that he had received (1 Corinthian 15:3). Where did he receive it? Scholars generally agree that Paul must have received this information when he "conferred" with St. Peter for 15 days in Jerusalem (Galatians 1:18). The Greek word translated "confer" is *historeo*, which means "to investigate" or "to acquire knowledge." Ancient historians used to sit at the outskirts of a city so that they could *historeo* with explorers upon their return. Similarly, Paul conferred with Peter for 15 days learning about Our Lord and the events that had transpired. When did this meeting occur? Scholars date around A.D. 35, which places St. Paul's list within five years of the resurrection.

If we stopped here, we would have more than ample grounds to dismiss any suggestion that our information about Christ's resurrection is too late. But there is more. If we dig a little deeper, we find something even more surprising. Scholars also note that this passage has a special form and structure, what is commonly called a literary form.

You may have noticed that Paul's list is punctuated by the word "that" or "after that" like bullet points:

"**that** Christ died…"

"**that** he was buried."

"**that** he was raised on the third day…"

"**that** he appeared to Kephas.…"

"**After that**, he appeared to more than five hundred…"

"**After that** he appeared to James, then to all the apostles…"

Scholars call this literary form a creedal statement, which makes it conducive to recitation and memorization. But it takes time for information to become formalized. If St. Paul received this information in its current state, it would mean that the list pre-dates our A.D. 35 date by a least a few years, which would bring the date within a year or two of Christ's resurrection. Such a short span of time should be more than sufficient to satisfy the most skeptical critic.

1 Timothy 4:14 - The Jewish Roots of the Laying on of Hands (July 22, 2016)

"Where in the Bible does it say that?" It's rare to find a New Testament passage that unpacks all the meaning and details of a given subject. Many times, it just assumes that the reader already knows the Old Testament background of the things and institutions that it mentions. Laying on of hands is a good example. The apostles laid hands on seven deacons (Acts 6:2-6); Paul laid hands on Timothy (1 Timothy 4:14). But what does this action mean? How did the early Christians understand it?

The earliest reference to the laying on of hands is found in Genesis 48:8-20, where Israel blesses Joseph's two sons, Ephraim and Manasseh, by putting a hand on each of their heads. This blessing is more than simply wishing them well. It's a bestowal of privileges due to the firstborn. Only in this case, Israel switches hands and gives the younger brother the blessing of the firstborn.

Moses also laid hands on Joshua at a very significant point in salvation history. When Moses knew that he was about to die, he prayed, "May the LORD, the God of the spirits of all mankind, set over the community a man who shall act as their leader in all things, to guide them in all their actions; that the LORD'S community may not be like sheep without a shepherd" (Numbers 27:15-23).

The Lord replied that Moses should "Take Joshua, son of Nun, a man of spirit, and lay your hand upon him. Have him stand in the presence of the priest Eleazar and of the whole community, and commission him before their eyes. Invest him with some of your own dignity, that the whole Israelite community may obey him." Moses did as God commanded.

In this instance, the laying on of hands was a sign that bestowed Moses' authority and dignity to Joshua. Moses did this before a large audience so that the people would know that Joshua had received this authority. In other words, Moses, by the laying on of hands, gave God's people a shepherd to lead them.

We learn elsewhere that the laying on of hands was more than just a symbol; it gave Joshua what he needed for his mission. Deuteronomy 34:9 says that after Moses died, "Now Joshua, son of Nun, was filled with the spirit of wisdom, since Moses had laid his hands upon him; and so the Israelites gave him their obedience, thus carrying out the LORD'S command to Moses." Why was Joshua "filled with the spirit of wisdom?" It was because "Moses had laid his hands upon him." Through the laying on of hands, God invested Joshua with what he needed to fulfill his calling.

With this background in mind, the New Testament references take on a new significance and help bring out certain details within St. Paul's exhortations to Timothy that we would have otherwise missed. For example, Paul exhorts Timothy to "… attend to the reading, exhortation, and teaching. Do not neglect the gift you have, which was conferred on you through the prophetic word with the imposition of hands of the presbyterate. Be diligent in these matters, be absorbed in them, so that your progress may be evident to everyone." Timothy's "gift" that was conferred by the laying on of hands echoes what we've seen concerning Moses laying hands on Joshua. Both Joshua and Timothy were invested with authority and the spiritual faculties to carry out their mission. Paul's exhortations to Timothy also show us something important about this gift: The graces it gives weren't automatic. Paul still needed to encourage Timothy to "stir into flame the gift of God" (2 Timothy 1:6), so that he could grow in these graces.

Although Paul's exhortations to Timothy applied to the sacrament of holy orders, it still applies to all of us in a general sense. All who are baptized and confirmed have received the gifts and graces to fulfill our calling as children of God, but we, too, have to grow in grace and "stir into flame the gift of God" that we have received.

Titus 1:12 - The Truth About Cretans (June 8, 2017)

"Cretans have always been liars, vicious beasts, and lazy gluttons."

Not exactly the type of slogan you'd find in an advertisement for the Island of Crete! And you probably wouldn't expect to find this derogatory remark in Scripture, either. But guess what? It is Scripture. Paul says this to Titus in Titus 1:12. Well, actually, that isn't exactly accurate. This is not Paul's saying, but rather Paul is quoting a philosopher. Let me give you the full quote:

"One of them, a prophet of their own, once said, 'Cretans have always been liars, vicious beasts, and lazy gluttons.'"

The background to this quotation is actually quite entertaining and something of an inside joke. First, who is the philosopher? It is the ancient Greek philosopher and poet Epimenides of Knossos (6th or 7th century B.C.). The phrase is quoted by Callimachus (c 300–240 B.C.) in the first half of his Hymn to Zeus, applying it to the

Cretan legend that the tomb of Zeus was on the island. The quote is:

"They fashioned a tomb for you, holy and high one, Cretans, always liars, evil beasts, idle bellies. But you are not dead: you live and abide forever, For in you we live and move and have our being."

Paul quotes the last line to the Greeks at the Areopagus in Acts 17:22-28:

> "... 'You Athenians, I see that in every respect you are very religious. For as I walked around looking carefully at your shrines, I even discovered an altar inscribed, 'To an Unknown God.' What therefore you unknowingly worship, I proclaim to you. The God who made the world and all that is in it, the Lord of heaven and earth, does not dwell in sanctuaries made by human hands, nor is he served by human hands because he needs anything. Rather it is he who gives to everyone life and breath and everything. He made from one the whole human race to dwell on the entire surface of the earth, and he fixed the ordered seasons and the boundaries of their regions, so that people might seek God, even perhaps grope for him and find him, though indeed he is not far from any one of us. For 'In him we live and move and have our being,' as even some of your poets have said, 'For we too are his offspring.'"

In a previous article, we noted that St. Paul grew up in a city named Tarsus. Tarsus was the ancient crossroad between the east and west, kind of like an ancient city of St. Louis. It had lots of commerce and it also was the center for stoic philosophy. Therefore, St. Paul was very familiar with pagan philosophy and had no problem pointing to Epimenides to open a conversation.

But did you notice in Titus 1:12 the unusual way Paul introduces his quote to Titus? He called the philosopher "a prophet *of their own*." What did he mean by "of their own?" Here is where things take a humorous turn. Epimenides of Knossos was from Crete! Therefore, Epimenides was making this derogatory remark, not only about his own people, but apparently about himself as well. Or did he?

Epimenides' statement has become famous as the "Epimenides paradox." It is a "self-referential" statement. When the Cretan Epimenides wrote that "Cretans always lie," we run into a conundrum. Is the statement true or false? If it is true that Cretans "always lie," than Epimenides (a Cretan) must be lying about Cretans always lying. Cretans, therefore, do not always lie. If the statement is false and Cretans do not always lie, then Epimenides of Crete is lying by saying that they do. There are a number of ways out of this paradox, such as the statement not being a statement of fact, but poetic hyperbole or that the falsity of "always lying" does not mean that they always tell the truth.

What's funny is that Paul, who certainly knew this paradox, concludes by saying in the very next verse: "That testimony is true" (Titus 1:13). I can only imagine Paul having a smile on his face when he wrote that last line.

The Epistle To the Hebrews

Who Wrote Hebrews? (June 22, 2017)

There is a letter in the New Testament that really isn't a letter at all. It is the Letter to the Hebrews (or "Hebrews" for short). Hebrews isn't written like a letter. It has no salutation at the beginning and no farewell at its conclusion. It just jumps right into the subject matter — which is too bad for historians, because the author never identifies himself.

Some early Church fathers believed the author to be St. Paul. The first Church historian, Eusebius, quotes Clement of Alexandria as saying:

> "And as for the Epistle to the Hebrews … indeed that it is Paul's, but that it was written for Hebrews in the Hebrew tongue, and that Luke, having carefully translated it, published it for the Greeks; hence, as a result of this translation, the same complexion of style is found in this Epistle and in the Acts: but that the [words] 'Paul an apostle' were naturally not prefixed …"

The earliest copies of Hebrews confirm Clement's statement. Paul's name does not appear in the title until the late second century or early third century.

Clement also noticed something that scholars notice today. The style of Hebrews is very different than Paul's other letters. Its Greek is very eloquent and polished, where his letters are not. This has led many scholars to doubt Paul's authorship. However, Clement recounts a tradition that says that Hebrews was said to be originally written in Hebrew, but translated into Greek by St. Luke, the author of the Gospel and the Acts of the Apostles.

Doubts about Paul's authorship continued after the second century. Tertullian, for example, believed Paul's companion Barnabas wrote Hebrews. Others thought it was written by Pope St. Clement of Rome. St. Jerome had doubts about Paul's authorship, although St. Augustine defended it.

Today, modern scholars still wrestle with the same questions as did the early Church. The differences in writing style, subject matter, and other items have turned many scholars against Paul being its author, but it is not clear exactly who else could have written it.

A few modern scholars thought Priscilla might have written it, although there is nothing to support this theory. Others point to Apollos, who is described in Acts 18:24-25:

> "A Jew named Apollos, a native of Alexandria, an eloquent speaker, arrived in Ephesus. He was an authority on the scriptures. He had been instructed in the Way of the Lord and, with ardent spirit, spoke and taught accurately about Jesus, although he knew only the baptism of John."

A scholar named E. H. Plumptre suggested that Apollos may be the author of both the Old Testament Book of Wisdom and the Letter to the Hebrews, claiming that Apollos wrote Wisdom while a Jew and wrote Hebrews after his conversion to Christianity. His theory rests mainly on the fact that Hebrews has dozens of parallels with the Book of Wisdom. Be that as it may, there still isn't anything to link Hebrews to Apollos. So who wrote Hebrews?

If you step back and look at all the possible candidates — Luke, Barnabas, Apollos, Priscilla and Clement — you'll notice that they all have one thing in common: They had contact with or were disciples of St. Paul. All of these different hypotheses ultimately boil down to a single common denominator: that St. Paul was in some way the source of the Letter to the Hebrews. Either he wrote the work and it was later reworked by another author who used Paul's teaching while writing Hebrews. One way or another, Hebrews and Paul are connected.

Regardless of how the Letter to the Hebrews is produced, its primary author is the Holy Spirit, and it is therefore authentic Scripture. In regards to its human author, however, we certainly can appreciate the beauty and its eloquence in which the author expressed himself, not to mention its powerful argumentation and depth of wisdom.

Hebrews 4:12 - Is the Bible a "Two-edged Sword"? (April 17, 2015)

Have you ever heard of a sword drill? A sword drill is a Bible quiz to help children find important passages in Scripture. Because Ephesians 6:17 calls the word of God the "sword of the spirit," these quizzes are called "sword drills."

Although the word of God is known as the "sword of the spirit," don't make the mistake of assuming that every passage that mentions the "word of God" and a "sword" is speaking about Scripture. This is especially true with one of the most commonly misinterpreted passages in Scripture, Hebrews 4:12, which reads:

> "Indeed, the word of God is living and effective, sharper than any two-edged sword, penetrating even between soul and spirit, joints and marrow, and able to discern reflections and thoughts of the heart."

This verse is often used by Protestants to argue that Christians don't need a teaching Church to understand the Bible, because Scripture itself is an active agent judging us and convicting our hearts of the truth.

One reason for this misinterpretation is that the reader fails to recognize that other things are called the "word of God" besides Scripture. For example, Our Lord Jesus Christ is called the Word of God in John 1:1. The same is true for the Apostles' preaching and the Gospel (1 Thessalonians 2:13). Which of these does Hebrews 4:12 have in mind? The answer is found in the context.

If you read the following two verses, you'll see exactly who Hebrews 4:12 is describing:

> "No creature is concealed from him, but everything is naked and exposed to the eyes of him to whom we must render an account. Therefore, since we have a great high priest who has passed through the heavens, Jesus, the Son of God, let us hold fast to our confession" (Hebrews 4:13-14).

These verses gives us three solid reasons why the "word of God" in Hebrews 4:12 cannot refer to Scripture. First, it says, "No creature is concealed from him." How can anyone conceal themselves from the Bible? That just doesn't make sense. Second, verse 13 speaks of everything being exposed to his eyes. A person has eyes, not a book. Third, all is "exposed to the eyes of him to whom we must render an account." At the end of time, do we render an account of our lives to the Bible or to Jesus? Obviously, Jesus. The last verse is the clincher, as it summarizes all that has just been said, "Therefore, since we have a great high priest … Jesus, the Son of God …" The word of God spoken of in Hebrews 4:12-14 is not the Bible, but Jesus Christ, the Word made flesh.

Still, someone may say Hebrews 4:12 is a rather odd description for Christ. We don't normally speak of Him in terms of one who is like a sword that can penetrate the deepest recesses of the heart. Where did the author of Hebrew get such images? The answer may be found in the book of Wisdom.

In Wisdom 18:14, Wisdom describes God's judgment on Egypt as, "Your all-powerful word from heaven's royal throne bounded, a fierce warrior, into the doomed land, bearing the sharp sword of your inexorable decree." Like Hebrews 4:12, the word of God is spoken of as an active personal agent who is associated with a sharp sword.

Earlier in the same book, the Wisdom of God is described in terms very similar to Hebrews 4:12:

> "… all-powerful, overseeing all, and penetrating through all spirits that are intelligent, pure, and

> altogether subtle. For wisdom ... pervades and penetrates all things (Wisdom 7:23-24)."

All of the main elements of Hebrews 4:12 (i.e., the word of God, the sharp sword, the ability to penetrate the deepest recesses of the heart) are found in reference to God's Wisdom in these two passages in the book of Wisdom. And we know that Christ is the Power and Wisdom of God (1 Corinthian 1:24), so Hebrews 4:12's description fits perfectly with Christ.

So the next time you encounter the "word of God" in Scripture, take a moment and study the context so you don't misinterpret what you're reading.

James 5:2-3 - Get Rid of Your Rusty Gold and Silver (Jan. 8, 2016)

One thing I advise people who attend my Bible studies not to do is to glance over difficulties because, more often than not, a little digging will reveal some interesting insights you otherwise would have missed. Take, for example, James 5:2-3:

> "Your wealth has rotted away, your clothes have become moth-eaten, your gold and silver have corroded, and that corrosion will be a testimony against you ..."

Hold on a second! Did he say "your gold and silver have corroded"? Here's the problem: Gold doesn't rust. In fact, gold doesn't naturally react to air or water. Why, then, would James speak of gold and silver rusting away? Clearly, there is more to this passage than meets the eye.

One possible solution might be found in the Greek word translated "corrupted" (Greek, *ios*). It's usually translated "poison" or "corruption." In regard to metal, it's usually translated "rust" or perhaps "tarnish." Anyone who owns silverware knows that silver tarnishes, so there's no problem here. But gold? Gold is the most non-reactive of all metals. It may darken a bit over time, but it doesn't tarnish, *per se*. Yet James causally speaks about "rust" and "gold" as if his readers would have immediately understood. What are we missing?

The answer, interestingly enough, is found not in the Hebrew Old Testament, but in an ancient Greek translation called the Septuagint and in a book that is not included in Rabbinical or Protestant Bibles. It's found in the Book of Sirach, 29:8-12, which reads:

> "To a poor man, however, be generous; keep him not waiting for your alms; Because of the precept, help the needy, and in their want, do not send them away empty-handed. Spend your money for your brother and friend, and hide it not under a stone to perish; Dispose of your treasure as the Most High commands, for that will profit you more than the gold. Store up almsgiving in your treasure house, and it will save you from every evil."

Sirach's point is that the true value of money is to serve others. Those who give alms to the poor, or a brother, or a friend, receive something more valuable than its value in bullion. It is deposited into "your treasure house, and it will save you from every evil." This personal treasure house contains not gold or silver, but what is pleasing to God so that "… it will save you from every evil." If you stockpile gold for your own benefit in your earthly treasure house (in this case under a stone), it will waste away.

Here we have the same odd idea we found in James, gold and silver rusting away. But Sirach is not giving us a lesson on metallurgy. He's teaching us about morals and the spiritual value of almsgiving. It is like storing up a heavenly treasure whereas selfish hording makes the gold and silver saved spiritually worthless.

Jesus echoes Sirach's teaching in Matthew 6:19-21, in which He instructs, "Do not store up for yourselves treasures on earth, where moth and decay destroy, and thieves break in and steal. But store up treasures in heaven, where neither moth nor decay destroys, nor thieves break in and steal. For where your treasure is, there also will your heart be."

Looking back at James 5:1-4, we see both Sirach and Matthew at work behind James' rusty gold:

> "Come now, you rich, weep and wail over your impending miseries. Your wealth has rotted away, your clothes have become moth-eaten, your gold and silver have corroded, and that corrosion will be a testimony against you; it will devour your flesh like a fire. You have stored up treasure for the last days."

Just as Sirach and Jesus teach that almsgiving and good works add to a heavenly treasure of reward before God, James teaches that the opposite is also true. The selfish use of money will not only become corrupt, but it will be added to a treasury of wrath for the Final Judgment so as to be a witness against its owner. The lesson for us is: Don't leave earth with rusty gold.

The Book of Revelation

A Revealing look at Revelation's Journey to the New Testament (July 8, 2016)

There is probably no other book in the Bible that is more disputed, controversial, and just plain difficult to understand than the book of Revelation. It shouldn't surprise us, therefore, that its place within the New Testament is also quite unusual.

Many of the books of the New Testament were immediately accepted as sacred Scripture by the early Christians. For example, there was never any doubt about the four Gospels' rightful place within the New Testament, although some later tried to add additional books that claimed to come from the Apostles. The same can be true for several of Paul's letters.

Other books had a more difficult time winning universal acceptance. Second Peter and the Second and Third Letter of John, for example, were first contested, but later these initial doubts faded and they remain in our Bibles. The acceptance of the book of Revelation was quite different.

Initially, the Book of Revelation's sacredness was accepted without difficulty. In fact, two prominent figures in the early Church, Irenaeus of Lyons (c. AD 180) and Tertullian (d. AD 220), affirmed its inspiration and used it as well. It would seem that by the end of the second Christian century, Revelation had a firm spot within the New Testament, but such was not the case.

The earliest doubts about the Book of Revelation started in the second century with a Roman priest named Caius. Caius believed Revelation to be a forgery of a heretic named Cerinthus, the main reason for which seems to be that Cerinthus taught that there would be an earthly kingdom after the Resurrection. Because the Book of Revelation could be read (or misread) to support such a view, Caius erroneously believed Cerinthus to be the author of the book.

However, this was just the first of several theories that associated Revelation with the early heresy. If you scan through religious programs on the radio or television, chances are you'll run across at least a few individuals who are propounding some pretty bizarre and far-fetched interpretations of Revelation. The same situation occurred in the early Church. Heretics sometimes anchored their bizarre and heretical end-time beliefs in passages from Revelation.

This didn't help Revelation's reputation. In fact, it led a few early Church Fathers, preferring to err on the side of safety, to omit the Book of Revelation from their New Testament canons.

Because heresies tended to affect only certain localities, doubts about Revelation were largely confined to the east. The rest of the Church, for the most part, didn't have a problem with the book or its place in the New Testament.

By the end of the fourth century, whatever doubts still lingered about the canonicity of Revelation were extinguished by two important local African councils, Hippo and Carthage. These councils re-affirmed the ancient Christian canon, and their decrees were affirmed by the pope. Thus, it became part of the law of the

Church, and from that point, Revelation's place in the New Testament was established. But the story wasn't over quite yet.

In the early 1500s, an Augustinian monk named Martin Luther once again contested Revelation, but on different grounds. By rejecting the authority of Church councils, Luther once again opened the question of the canon. In addition to rejecting the seven deuterocanonical books of the Old Testament, Luther also cast doubts on the Deuterocanon of the New Testament (i.e., James, Hebrews, 2nd and 3rd John, Jude and Revelation).

In his 1522 preface to Revelation, Luther wrote, "…let everyone think of it as his own spirit leads him. My spirit cannot accommodate itself to this book. For me this is reason enough not to think highly of it: Christ is neither taught nor known in it … Therefore I stick to the books which present Christ to me clearly and purely." However, Luther's theological reservations about the New Testament Deuterocanon were soon abandoned and the Book of Revelation remained in Protestant Bibles.

Revelation 2:17- Jesus and the Sign of the "Hidden Manna" (April 15, 2016)

After the exodus from Egypt, God fed his people with a mysterious food called manna. Its name comes from the Hebrew word *man*, which means "what?" In other words, this mysterious food is essentially called "What is it?" When the people asked this question to Moses, he simply replied, "This is the bread which the LORD has given you to eat" (Exodus 16:15).

Manna looked like thin flakes that formed on the ground, much like frost (Exodus 16:14-15), and it tasted like honey or fresh oil (Exodus 16:31, Numbers 11:8). The Israelites were allowed to gather manna each day to eat, one portion per person, but no matter how much or how little they gathered, each had enough to eat (Exodus 16:18). Extra manna could not be kept for the next day, except on Friday. Because the Israelite's could not work on the Sabbath, they were allowed to gather twice as much manna on Friday so they could eat it on the Sabbath.

We are familiar with the story of the manna because of its connection with the Eucharist. After the multiplication of the loaves, the people asked Jesus, "…What sign can you do, that we may see and believe in you? What can you do? Our ancestors ate manna in the desert, as it is written: 'He gave them bread from heaven to eat'" (John 6:30-31). Jesus replies that he is the living bread that comes down from heaven (John 6:35) that is he is the true manna.

Jesus also speaks of manna in the book of Revelation. In Revelation 2:17, Jesus says, "To the victor I shall give some of the hidden manna…" What's curious is his description, "hidden manna." *Hidden* manna? The manna wasn't hidden. The Israelite's gathered it and ate it in their homes. The manna was very public. What does Jesus mean by the "hidden manna?"

Most people are not aware that there was manna that was hidden from the public. God told Moses to take some of the manna and put it into an urn and place it before Him in the Tabernacle (Exodus 16:32-34). This portion of hidden manna was to be saved for future generations. Therefore, Moses placed it inside the Ark of the Covenant along with the Ten Commandments and Aaron's rod

(Hebrews 9:4). Exodus does not tell us when the future generations will receive this hidden manna. There was an expectation, however, that when the messiah came he would provide future generations with manna.

A non-biblical Jewish writing called Second Baruch says this about the messiah:

> "And it shall come to pass when all is accomplished that was to come to pass in those parts, that the Messiah shall then begin to be revealed. ... And it shall come to pass at that self-same time that the treasury of manna shall again descend from on high, and they will eat of it in those years, because these are they who have come to the consummation of time. And it shall come to pass after these things, when the time of the advent of the Messiah is fulfilled, that He shall return in glory" (2 Baruch 29:2, 8, 30:1).

The Jews who asked Jesus for a sign like Moses and the manna in John 6 probably had this idea in mind. I'm sure they didn't expect his response: "I am the bread of life. Your ancestors ate the manna in the desert, but they died; this is the bread that comes down from heaven so that one may eat it and not die" (John 6:48-50).

Jesus does bring down from heaven the "treasury of manna" put away for future generations in the Eucharist, where he is still hidden under the appearances of bread and wine. Ultimately, the Eucharist is a foretaste of the messianic banquet at the end of time (Revelation 19:9). Only then will the manna not be hidden and we "will see him as he is" (1 John 3:2). Until then, we feed on the hidden manna that Christ gives us in the Eucharist.

Revelation 1:17 (also Revelation 21:6-7) - Who is the Alpha and the Omega? (May 27, 2016)

Have you ever heard someone say, "We're going to cover everything from A to Z?" The phrase might be more biblical than you think. If you replace the first and last letters of the English alphabet with the Greek, what do you get? Alpha and Omega.

The Alpha and the Omega might sound familiar. These two Greek letters are sometimes found on priestly vestments or written on an icon; even Easter candles have these two letters. But do you know the biblical background and what they signify?

As I implied, "the Alpha and the Omega" is a Greek way of saying "A to Z." It means essentially "from the beginning to the end" of something, as when someone says, "I followed the directions from A to Z." It means every step from the first step to the last.

The Old Testament expresses the same idea using the phrase "first and last." It is most commonly used to describe the contents of an account of someone. For example, 1 Chronicles 29:29 says, "Now the deeds of King David, first and last, can be found written in the history of Samuel ..." The same expression is used to describe the acts of Solomon (2 Chronicles 9:29), Rehoboam (2 Chronicles 12:15), Asa (2 Chronicles 16:11), Jehoshaphat (2 Chronicles 20:23), Amaziah (2 Chronicles 25:26), and Uzziah (2 Chronicles 26:22). In this context, "first and last" denotes the fullness or completeness of the account.

The phrase, however, takes on a few new nuances in Isaiah. For example, God says of Himself in Isaiah 41:4, "Who has performed these deeds? He who has called forth the generations since the beginning. I, the LORD, am the first, and with the last I will also be." He likewise says in Isaiah 48:12–13, "Listen to me, Jacob, Israel, whom I named! I, it is I who am the first, and also the last am I. Yes, my hand laid the foundations of the earth; my right hand spread out the heavens. When I call them, they stand forth at once."

In both instances, the "first and last" signifies that God is beyond the totality of all things. Because there is nothing before Him (being the first) and nothing after Him (since He is the last), there can be nothing that supersedes Him. He is Almighty. It also shows that God is both the origin and the destiny of all things.

Isaiah 44:6 adds yet one more shade of meaning when God says, "I am the first and I am the last; there is no God but me." Being the first and the last, God is utterly unique. There can be no other like Him.

The Book of Revelation also applies "first and last" and "the Alpha and Omega" to Jesus. Jesus says in Revelation 1:8, "'I am the Alpha and the Omega,' says the Lord God, 'the one who is and who was and who is to come, the almighty.'" Being the Alpha and the Omega, first and last, Jesus is the Almighty.

In Revelation 1:17, Jesus tells John, "Do not be afraid. I am the first and the last…" John later introduces Jesus' words to the church in Smyrna as, "The first and the last, who once died but came to life, says this.…'" (Revelation 2:8). Finally, Jesus says in Revelation 22:12-13, "Behold, I am coming soon … I am the

Alpha and the Omega, the first and the last, the beginning and the end."

What's curious is that God speaks only once in the entire book of Revelation. What did He say? "I (am) the Alpha and the Omega, the beginning and the end ... " (Revelation 21:6-7). If God the Father is the Alpha and the Omega, the beginning and end, and Jesus is the Alpha and the Omega, the beginning and end, it suggests that two persons, the Father and the Son, are the one unique Alpha and the Omega, the origin and destiny of all things, the Almighty. These verses might not be an "A to Z" description of the Trinity (since we haven't mentioned the Holy Spirit), but they are a good start.

Revelation 13:18 - The Number of the Beast: What's Behind "666"? (May 8, 2017)

The number 666 appears all over the place, from horror movies to the markings on a popular energy drink. But what is so special about this number?

Those familiar with the Book of Revelation know that this is a number of the beast. In chapter 13, Revelation speaks about how the beast that will arise and perform miracles that will deceive the inhabitants of the earth. No one was allowed to buy or sell unless they had the image of the beast stamped on their right hands or their foreheads. The chapter closes with the following statement:

> "Wisdom is needed here; one who understands can calculate the number of the beast, for it is a

number that stands for a person. His number is six hundred and sixty-six" (Revelation 13:18).

What does it mean that the number "stands for the person"? Ancient languages didn't use numbers; they used letters. Different letters were assigned certain numeric values, such as the case with Roman numerals. The letter "I" has the value of one and "V" has the value of five and so on. This means that names that contain letters with numeric values can add up to a number, and according to Revelation, the beast's name adds up to 666.

I'm sorry to disappoint you, but there's not even room in this article to identify the beast, per se. Instead, we are going to look at the biblical background of this number, which, in some ways, is just as fascinating.

Scripture often associates ideas with numbers. For example, the number seven seems to be closely associated with the sense of covenant, fullness and completeness. For example, God created in six days and rested on the seventh. The seventh day has the sense of completeness and it is also the Sabbath, the covenant day of rest. Likewise, Abraham sacrificed seven ewe lambs to make a covenant at Beersheba in Genesis 21. We also see the same sense of completeness in Psalm 12:6, which reads: "The words of the Lord are pure words; As silver tried in a furnace on the earth, refined seven times." Refining silver seven times makes it most pure. The number six is obviously one short of seven. It therefore carries a sense of incompleteness and not being of a covenant.

The fact that six is repeated three times is also significant. It is sometimes thought that Hebrew didn't have a way to express superlatives (that something is the best), so it repeats it three times.

This is not true, however. This doesn't mean that the threefold repetition is meaningless. Scripture often associates three with God. For example, the Shema "Hear, O Isreal: the LORD our GOD, the LORD is one" mentions God three times. God is called "Holy" three times (Isaiah 6:3-4, Revelation 4:8) and there are three persons in the blessed Trinity (Matthew 28:19). The thrice repeated six could be seen as a blasphemous mocking of God, which certainly fits the context of Revelation 13.

But what about six-hundred and sixty six? Is there any biblical precedence for this number? It occurs in two contexts: The first is in regard to the number of sons of Adonikam in Ezra 2:13, but this is likely a scribal error (cf. Nehemiah 7:18-19). The second time 666 appears is in the life of King Solomon.

King Solomon? How could Solomon possibly be associated with someone like the beast? As you probably know, Solomon started out good, but he had a great fall. Deuteronomy 17:14-17 commanded the kings not to multiply armies (horses), foreign alliances (wives), or accumulate wealth. Solomon, despite his great gift of wisdom, violated all three of these restrictions and during the peak of his power received 666 talents of gold in a single year (1 Kings 10:14; 2 Chronicles 9:13). Solomon's excesses led to oppressive taxation and eventually a revolt that broke apart his father's kingdom. Revelation 13:18 may have had this in mind when it instructs the reader, "Wisdom is needed here," since Solomon was known for his wisdom. The beast, whoever he was, must have been very much like Solomon, having massive armies, foreign alliances and wealth.

Revelation 13:18 - Does "666" Add Up To Nero? (May 18, 2017)

One of the most enigmatic passages in the book of Revelation is the number of the name of the beast — "666." Popular culture has embraced this number and used it for everything from horror movies to energy drinks, but what does it mean? Who is "666"?

In the last article, we saw how the number could symbolically represent imperfection or perhaps even a mocking of the Holy Trinity. But the biblical background to "666" tied into King Solomon, who at the height of his power received 666 talents of gold. We noted that Solomon was a type of Christ. He was the son of David and the builder of the temple. However, Solomon transgressed God's command to kings not to have larger armies, many foreign alliances, or to multiply gold. Therefore, the number 666 could represent a ruler who has unbridled power.

With this background in mind, let's try to give at least one viable answer to who exactly John was identifying with "666." I approach this question with some trepidation because there is no other book in the Bible more difficult to interpret than Revelation. In fact, one of the very first articles I wrote for *The Michigan Catholic* was to outline the different approaches to this book.

Some believe Revelation speaks about events that largely had already occurred. Others believe it speaks only about future events. Still others see it a purely symbolic representation of the battle between good and evil that occurs in every age. There are also approaches that combine the ones above.

Where does this leave us? If Revelation is speaking of the beast as someone who has already come, the best candidate appears to be Nero Caesar (reigned AD 54-68).

Revelation 13:8 says, "Wisdom is needed here; one who understands can calculate the number of the beast, for it is a number that stands for a person. His number is six hundred and sixty-six."

The Greek name "Nero Caesar" put into Hebrew letters is *NRON QSRN*, which adds up to six hundred and sixty-six. If this were all we had to go on, then Nero would not be any more likely a candidate than any other name that could add up to this number, but there is one more piece of evidence that points to Nero.

We learn from the early Church father Irenaeus of Lyons that in his day (c. AD 180) the reading "666" was "... found in all the most approved and ancient copies" (*Against Heresies*, 5, 30, 1), but he doesn't tell us what number the minority manuscripts give. There is manuscript evidence that the alternative number is "616." But why this second number? Where did it come from?

It's possible that the second number comes from the Latin version of Nero's name, which, when put into Hebrew letters drops the second "N" (Hebrew, *Nun*) so that it reads, NRO QSR instead of NRON QSR. Since "N" *Nun*) has the value of "50." The Greek version of his name when put into Hebrew letters has the value of 666, while the Latin version has the value of 616.

Nero also seems to be a likely candidate in that Revelation 13:3 speaks about the beast having one head that "... seemed to have been mortally wounded, but this mortal wound was healed. Fascinated, the whole world followed after the beast." Roman historians report that after Nero committed suicide in AD 68, there was a widespread belief — possibly generated through the prediction of a group of astrologers — that Nero was not dead but would return to power soon. After Nero's death, there were three imposters who pretended to be "*Nero Redivivdus*" (Nero reborn).

All this being said, its value depends on how one approaches Revelation. If you believe that Revelation speaks exclusively of the future, then Nero obviously isn't a candidate. Otherwise, everything adds up to Nero.

Other Books and Resources by Gary Michuta

Hostile Witnesses: How The Historic Enemies of the Church Prove Christianity

15 Myths, Mistakes and Misrepresentations About The Deuterocanon

The Case for the Deuterocanon: Evidence and Arguments

Making Sense of Mary

How to Wolf-Proof Your Kids: A Practical Guide To Keeping Your Kids Catholic

Why Catholic Bibles Are Bigger: The Untold Story of the Lost Books of the Protestant Bible

The Gospel According to James McCarthy: A Catholic Answer to James McCarthy's "The Gospel According to Rome"

CD SETS

Defending the Faith Series Volumes 1-5 (Is Salvation Guaranteed? / Is Sacred Tradition Necessary? / From Peter to Papacy / The Sacrifice of the Mass / Mary: Unveiling the Blessed Virgin's Role in God Plan of Redemption)

An Unexpected Calling / Does Romans Teach Justification Apart from Works? (Michuta v. Kliewer) / The Claims of Christ and the Reliability of the Gospels / The Jehovah's Witnesses Explained: A Catholic Look at the Watchtower's History and Doctrine

www.GaryMichuta.com

www.HandsOnApologetics.com

Made in the USA
Las Vegas, NV
21 September 2021